Immortality

By
Draja Mickaharic

Lulu, USA

First Published in 2007 by
Lulu, Inc.
860 Aviation Parkway   Suite 300
Morrisville, NC   27560
919-459-5858
www.Lulu.com

© 2007 by Draja Mickaharic & John M. Hansen
All rights reserved.

ISBN: 978-1-4303-1751-7
LCCN

Printed in the United States of America

DEDICATION

This book is sincerely dedicated to my
good friend, and fellow magician,
Mishka N. who I am sure will be
embarrassed by the dedication

D. M.

CONTENTS

I	An Introduction And Forewarning	1
II	On Becoming Immortal	5
III	Betty And Gloria	23
IV	Varmus	43
V	Tale Of The Coachman Of Paris	79
VI	A Tale Of The Elixir Of Life	89
VII	A Tale Of The Wandering Jew	101
VIII	Other Immortals	111
IX	Processes Of Immortality	117

PREFACE

This work contains some stories and tales of the very long-lived, along with some information about gaining or continuing a long life. This is all information I have gathered over the years, and I present it here for your entertainment and amusement.

This book is not to be considered either a guide to becoming immortal or an encouragement to search out such a guide. Indeed, although these are all stories I have heard being presented as if they were truth, it would be best if you consider this work to just be a pleasant fiction.

~

By way of acknowledgment, I would like to express my grateful appreciation to all of those people who have told me the stories of their very interesting lives, and who, by necessity, must remain unknown. I thank them for extending their confidence to me, and I acknowledge their desire for privacy in these matters.

1

An Introduction and Forewarning

    I must warn the potential reader, this is not a book revealing the secret of how to become immortal. Were it even possible for me to write such a work, I am not sure that I should wish to do so. As one ages, it is natural their desire for life seems to dim, they look forward to the eternal peace that death offers. Thus, in time, the idea of immortality loses most of its charm.
    Indeed, this book is only a retelling, in a much fuller and more dramatic form, of some of the several curious stories concerning immortality I have heard in the course of my rather long life. These stories have all interested me, and I hope they also interest you.
    As a consultant dealing in practical matters often called occult, I have heard all kinds of stories, and have become privy to the secrets of a great many people. I hesitate to pass to my grave without revealing some of the more interesting of these secrets to the world, although without revealing the source from which I learned them. Naturally, I have carefully concealed all of those traces possibly identifying any people who might be involved in these tales. I have also changed the location of every person, town, or village in these stories, to make those references

IMMORTALITY

even more unidentifiable. Of course, those activities occurring near my home in New York City are identified as happening there. New York City is large enough to conceal any number of things under its quite ample wings, as it has always done in the past, and undoubtedly will continue to do in the future.

I hope the reader enjoys these stories, although none of them promise immortality, or even relief from the process of aging. Relief from the aging process is something that all of us seek, once we pass about fifty years of age. Being well past that age, I can assure you that the process of aging does not relent. Age withers, and does not restore.

~

I believe it was about 1959, when I first began writing these tales down. They have all been rewritten over the years, and were not put into final form by myself until late in 1998. I handed the finished manuscript over to a friend, who I am sure will change the words around to suit himself. This is called editing, and is something every author must put up with.

My friend has my received permission to make these changes, as without his generous assistance, these words would likely never see the light of day.

I do hope you enjoy these tales of those who are supposedly long lived. I certainly enjoyed hearing them when I first encountered them. I must say in all honesty that I really do not know what to think of these stories. As I mention later, it seems to me that one of these methods of extending one's life is entirely possible. I am not at all certain that I would wish to try it, but there are certain traces of information I have come across indicating to me that it is something that could actually be accomplished. I am very well aware that projecting out of the body into the physical world is quite possible for many people.

Should someone have succeeded in extending his or her life by use of the projection method mentioned, I would be delight to hear about their experiences from them. I should also add that the projection method, mentioned in two of these sto-

AN INTRODUCTION AND FOREWARNING

ries, is not one limited to the male sex, which historically is the sex these other life extension methods have been designed for.

Having had some conversations with people dealing with organ transplants, a friend of mine is an anesthesiologist, while the daughter of one of my friends is a nurse anesthetist; I have heard several stories of the various personality changes that have taken place in those who have received these transplants. I go into this in a bit more detail later on, but I will say now that these reported personality changes are another evidence to me that the method of projection mentioned in two of these stories is hardly impossible. I will also add that an Indian Yoga master who I attempted to discuss this with said that he could only talk of such things to someone who was at an equal level of initiation in the Yoga society he belonged to.

Learning these things does make me wonder.

At my age, writing and watching the television, whose advertisements annoy me to an incredible degree, are my primary recreation. I sincerely hope you enjoy reading my words as much as I enjoy writing them. I also wish to thank you for buying this book, whose purchase acts to supplement the meager social security income I receive in my retirement.

My very best wishes for your reading pleasure
Draja Mickaharic

IMMORTALITY

On Becoming Immortal

It would seem to be a desire of many people to become immortal. I understand there are now several organizations, both non-profit and commercial, which are dedicated to attaining this goal. Concerning this desire, I have heard that someone has done a statistical study, which shows it is statistically unlikely for any human being to live more than six hundred years. His figures seem to indicate that within such a time span, the person would have had to encounter a fatal accident of some kind.

Compared to the biblically mentioned 'three score and ten years' life span, supposedly granted the average person, a life span of six hundred years, more than eight and a half times as long as the biblical allowance, would probably seem as if it were immortality to most people. Although when many people cam to the end of their vastly increased life span, they might wish to extend it even further.

I believe those people who seek only entertainment and pleasure would have a great deal of difficulty in enjoying a life of such great length. I would think this was especially so, if their body continued to degenerate into the mass of aches and pains I have discovered from my own experience the body rapidly accumulates when it is approaching, and passes, the biblical allowance of seventy years. When increased age brings increased debility, we must think that death has no longer become a problem, but is now a blessing.

Aside from the chance of danger and the difficulties of aging, there is also the mental difficulty of adapting to the many cultural and technological changes any society passes through. The world today is a very different place than it was six hundred years ago, or even a hundred years ago. Is it not likely someone caught into the life of the so called immortal six hundred years ago, might long for death, simply to be spared having to pass through more traumatic cultural and social changes in their extended life time? Surely, the changes of the last six hundred years would have been a great mental or psychic shock to the person who has lived through them. We might call this the psychological problem of living to a great age. I see it as a practical difficulty as well. I believe few people are sufficiently mentally flexible to pass through such social and cultural changes without becoming either quite emotionally distressed, or possibly even becoming severely mentally unstable.

Yet, the constant human desire seems to be for immortality, enjoyed with the vigor of youth and good, if not perfect, health. Naturally, this desired state also assumes there are sufficient funds to ease ones life, preferably in former times as a member of the nobility, or today, being one of the few truly idle rich. This ideal usually has the idle dreamer seeking to become one of the jet set globetrotting very wealthy. Despite this being their desired goal, it would seem this would be an unlikely thing for the so-called immortal, or anyone else, to actually find. I believe being an immortal, or even having a very long-lived life, would likely present more upset than it would grant ease.

Supposing one was a highly skilled craftsman in the 1400's, and suddenly they were somehow made immortal. How much of their craftsmanship would last through the many years, or the centuries, of their extended life? I would think the life of a professional man would be even more difficult. How many years would it be before an immortal physician or attorney would have to be retrained? What profession would they then follow?

So there are problems of living a life involved in the search for immortality, problems that are certainly not under the control of the individual who is supposedly becoming ageless. One great difficulty is the age at which the person becomes immortal. If they become immortal when they are very young, the person may find they have to be cared for by others. People would not take them seriously, and others, who may be much younger than the immortal is chronologically, would not treat them as a mature human being. Of course, should the individual become immortal at too old an age, it is likely their faculties would have faded to such an extent a boon of immortality would present a greater burden to them than simply facing and accepting their approaching death.

I know that I would have greatly resented being made immortal, had it happened at fifty, much less at seventy or eighty. At those ages it is best to let death become a friend, rather than seek to extend your life. One must honestly admit to themselves when the greater joys of youth have passed forever.

There are three primary causes of death, aging, disease, and trauma. Should we defeat aging, disease and trauma are still to be faced. I beleive this is why those fictional immortal vampires, concerning whom Ms. Anne Rice has written, are also granted freedom from disease in her stories.

I have heard those who have taken the so-called alchemical elixir of immortality are also free from fear of aging, as well as fears of either disease or poisoning. This leaves death by physical trauma as the one sure and certain event that would put an end to an unusually long life. Of course, such dangerous physical trauma is more likely among those working in difficult and hazardous occupations, or serving in the military services. I would think those who are immortals would strive hard to avoid exposure to any physical conflict or personal conflict. I should think that any immortal would be one of the most cautious and safety conscious of men.

IMMORTALITY

The chance of military conscription is another difficulty facing the person who desires to be immortal. Obviously, the military would like to have someone who is comfortably healthy and seems not to age, but this does not say they would care to ever release them to civilian life, to say nothing at all of the person's chances of being killed or physically injured while in either the military or naval service. The military is famous for either ignoring those oddities among their ranks, or should they notice them, for pulling them out for close, and often physically damaging study. This study is frequently accomplished to the grave and even permanent detriment of the person themselves.

Thus, the chance of an unwelcome military conscription is another difficulty facing the person who desires to become long-lived or immortal, despite any thoughts to the contrary. Saying you have moral objections to military service does not always operate to your benefit, as often this is an excuse for the conscripting authority to put the supposed conscientious objector to either enforced physical labor of the lowest kind, or even give them a painful death. Military conscription is one difficulty, which just might put a quick, and quite possibly a painful end to the otherwise long-lived individual.

Of course, this fear of conscription is only a risk to those of vital years, the very young and the aged have nothing to worry about from the act of legal conscription, or even the beat of the press gang's drum. However, in lands where universal military service is the rule, there is always this difficulty to be faced by anyone of youthful or vital appearance, regardless of their true age.

However, if you do not become immortal when you are in those years when health and vitality are at their prime, what is the sense of the matter? Who would wish to begin an immortal life in their sixties, with an aged and debilitated body, and having the prospect of a long cavern of a thousand years to look forward to, living through time being already aged, and slowly aging further? The prospect of supposed eternal life would seem then to be a worse sentence than one of immediate death.

ON BECOMING IMMORTAL

Immortality, when one is in their early or mid twenties is one thing. However, immortality beginning at an advanced age is something I think would be more to be feared than desired. Yet there are stories of those who have become immortal at a rather advance age, and who have just disappeared from the ken of mankind due to some social upset, possibly one for which they were not prepared. The tale of the Coachman of Paris, which I give below, is one such story. I have heard of a very few others, going along much the same lines.

The classic case of the alchemical immortal is the tale of the alchemist Flamel and his wife Pernelle, who supposedly perishing in their fifties, (although some say their eighties) were replaced by logs, discovered in their caskets, when the caskets were opened a century or so after their supposed deaths.

Of course, there are other stories of those who supposedly are immortal, or whom some people of their time believed to be immortal, or at the very least, were believed by many people to be immortal. The tales of the fabulous Count St. Germain is but one of the better known of these supposed immortals. This famous nobleman is supposedly still alive, his death in Schleswig on February 27th 1784, witnessed and recorded by the attending physician, not withstanding.

Other stories tell of those whom were once known many years ago appearing seemingly un-aged in later times, such as the well known French Alchemist Flamel, who was supposedly met a century or so after his recorded death, by someone who met him in Turkey. The person said that he recognized the count from a portrait. A similar tale is told of the Count St. Germain, who was said to have been seen in the mid eighteen hundreds by someone who had known him when he was alive.

These tales come to us from all parts of the world. There is the recurring story or tale of the man in China who was recorded as being a professor of herbal medicine at a remote university for a period of over two hundred years. Not an immortal possibly, but certainly smacking of something of at least a rather similar nature.

IMMORTALITY

A well-known, although rare, medical syndrome, Hutchinson - Gilford Progeria, results in the premature rapid aging, as well as the early death of the unfortunate individual who is afflicted with this genetic condition. I believe it possible the obverse of this condition may exist. This would be a genetic condition in which the process of aging is greatly slowed, and death is long postponed. The afflicted person would live far longer than their biblical span of three score and ten years. Of course, misadventure and accident would put paid to any adventuring in their life, either in their normal life span, or during the years, the genetic syndrome might have extended their life beyond the normal. To my mind, it is quite likely some, if not most, of the reported conditions of those who have reportedly lived far beyond their normal life spans may relate to those having this unusual genetic condition. Of course, the flow of life being what it is, it is unlikely anyone, realizing they are only slowly ageing, and will potentially live long beyond the normal span, would be interested in reporting this condition to the medical authorities. They would probably consider it simply a boon, a preserver of the active years of their life. This would be particularly true if their active life in their apparent twenties, thirties, and forties, were extended for a few decades, or possibly even for a far longer span. Considering the most common reports of longevity, it might well be this medical obverse of early aging progeria is actually the truth of the matter.

We might also cautiously note that it is reported of those few people of whom we have heard tales concerning their apparent long life, such as stories of the famous Count St. Germain, that they always ate separately and of a meal of their own devising and preparation. The Count was said to use a purge of elder flowers, fennel, and senna pods, soaked in spirits of wine, or brandy. This would be a particularly strong laxative.

In addition, it was said that he was only took oatmeal as his food, which he prepared himself. This special diet might be a necessity in the encouragement of long life, or it might be a necessity because of the oddity of the genetic fluke we are now assuming is what prolongs both the life and vigor of the one so afflicted.

I must reveal I have found no record of anyone ever saying they actually witnessed the famous count St. Germain actually ever eating anything at all. Objective research into the lives of those few reasonably public individuals, who have been reported to live for long centuries, might reveal the truth of this matter. Of course, the truth is seldom as interesting as the romance, so we must be cautious about being too forward about exposing those findings disagreeing radically with the romantic stories and legends we have heard about these very rare chronological wonders. Fantasy is always more interesting than the prosaic tales of the daily reality of our lives.

After all, we remember Juan Ponce de Leon for his unsuccessful search for the fountain of youth, when he traveled to Florida in 1513. How many people recall that he had a rather glamorous, adventurous, and a very active life, before he began his futile search for immortality?

What of these marvelous tales of the alchemist's miraculous elixir of life, said to prolong the lives of those whom have had access to it? No one knows what has happened to those whom were properly dosed with this substance, but the tales I have heard concerning its application all agree in stating that improper overdosing invariably causes rapid if not an instant death. Should such a miraculous potent actually exist, and in this realm of conjecture we are exploring, we need not doubt it does, it is certainly out of reach of those of us who are not either alchemists or the very close associates of one of these most interesting people.

In the meantime, we have the stories of the supposedly empty graves of Nicolas Flamel and his wife to console us as to the possible reality of these tales of the alchemist's draught. There are several other similar stories, such as the equally empty grave of the beheaded Vald the Impaler, the original Count Dracula. Should we wish to investigate the matter even further, there are actually quite a number of these stories of empty

IMMORTALITY

graves, and tales of people who were supposedly dead being seen several decades, or even many centuries, after their recorded demise. Of course, stories, myths, romance, and conjecture are always preferable to the pragmatic realities of the always-harsh physical world. The physical proof that objective truth demands is never quite forthcoming in these instances.

It would seem from the example of Flamel one must first be a gold making alchemist before the possibility of gaining eternal life by the alchemical tincture of immortality is to be contemplated. However, there are other cases, such as the coachman of Paris, who was said to have been made immortal quite accidentally some years before the French Revolution. No alchemist he, but an illiterate attendant upon the horse drawn coach of his employer. His very interesting story, told to me by a wealthy man who vainly sought immortality for himself, follows here in its turn.

Thus, we have another of these endless oddities, worthy of objective investigation by those who have the education, the means, and the time, to do so. What comes of this research, which must first be done in libraries, and only later in the flesh, will be of interest to those who have no interest in alchemy, but seek only to live vitally forever, or for at least some years, or a few decades, beyond their naturally allotted lifespan.

I once read somewhere information concerning various magical methods of extending one's life. I was amazed the book had been published, and unfortunately, in my advanced age, and with now a quite slippery memory, I have no idea where the book is, or even if I still have it. However, the methods mentioned in the book are reasonably well known to me from numerous other sources, so I shall explain them all below. However, in honesty I must add I do not believe anyone is likely to successfully accomplish any of these interesting techniques in this world of impatience, change, turmoil, and strife.

I will mention the assumption being made in all of these methods is that it is a man who is extending his life, so obviously these techniques have all been designed for a male.

ON BECOMING IMMORTAL

Similar techniques would have to be employed should it be a female who is desirous of extending her life. This first technique would probably have to be modified, but likely only slightly. However, as I seriously doubt the first technique would actually work in any event, this is of little practical concern for those who would actually seek to extend their life.

The First Method

If you are still full of vital energy, and have around yourself a circle of associates whom you can absolutely trust, the following method is supposedly the safest and the most productive. However, as I say, I doubt it would actually work to produce the results desired, as unfortunately, it leaves a great deal to those you trust in this endeavor, as well as to the random winds of fate and chance.

According to this schema of life preservation, the man who wishes to prolong his life has intercourse with a fertile woman, and holding her in his arms until, as his sperm joins her egg, he deliberately and consciously passes from life to death. The spirit of the deceased then husbands the growing fertile egg in her womb until it develops into the male child, which is to become the vessel of his own reincarnation. The child being born, the man's trusted associates provide for it, educating it, and gradually recalling to the growing child all of the details of its previous life. In time, near or after the child enters into puberty, the man is said to resume the full memory of its previous life. By the time the child passes through puberty, he has become himself once again, having all of those powers the man had when he voluntarily perished, to be reborn anew as himself in a new body.

Naturally, funds, preparation, isolation, and great caution, would all be required to accomplish this remarkable transfer of life from one body to another. As I said, this places a great weight on the associates of the man, as well as reliance that the winds of change shall not disturb this plan. It is the reliance on the fates that leads me to believe this technique would be unsuccessful if it were actually ever attempted.

Having associates whom can be trusted in this delicate a matter would seem to be one of the prime difficulties of the process. After all, we are considering a process taking between fifteen to twenty years to bring to completion. Having funds to cover for such a long time, as well as having associates who are to be so completely trusted, especially over so long a time would seem to be difficult. Thus, this method seems to me to be impractical if not almost impossible. However, these obstacles aside, it would seem this method is rather well known. I wonder if it has actually ever been successfully used. Personally, people being what they are, I would have my doubts it ever has been used successfully by anyone. Although some adventurous person may have attempted to find immortality through this process, I consider it unlikely they would succeed.

I wonder what would happen if the child were born, but somehow not educated or restored to his former estate. Would there be a lingering suspicion of its former life? Would there be resentment, or even a desire for vengeance against the person's formerly trusted associates who had failed him in some way? Interesting questions indeed. I have no answer to any of them.

A similar method involves the person who wishes to become immortal committing suicide as a friend impregnates a willing and fertile woman who will later bear the hopeful immortal as her child. I would think this would be even more hazardous, as I know no one who would wish to have the difficulty of explaining the suicide to the authorities. Suicide leaves traces, and it is no longer possible to hide bodies under the nearest bush. There is also the esoteric question as to whether or not it is actually possible for a suicide to reincarnate under these circumstances. Once again, I doubt this method has ever succeeded, although it may well have been tried. There are those in this world who will attempt anything to achieve their desires, no matter how exotic these desires might be.

ON BECOMING IMMORTAL

There are also those stories purporting to tell of reincarnation, usually coming from India, or the Middle East, in which the person is reincarnated after they die in another village. They often return to their original village, meet their former wife or husband, who after speaking with them confirms this supposed event. As I recall, all of these stories seem to be the tales of those who were born in the rural villages or the tribal areas of India, the Middle East, or in some other rural part of the world. These do not ever seem to be deliberately planned reincarnations rather. They always seem to be just something that happened to the person.

While this does not make me doubt these stories, I do find it interesting to discover that the ones who are reborn seem to always be either peasant farmers or highly ranked priests and religious luminaries, such as one of the reincarnated Lamas of Tibet. Of course, this last is another far better known instance of this reincarnation process.

These tales make me wonder if it is possible to enter into death and go through the process of pregnancy and birth while continuing to carry all of your former memories and experiences with you. This is essentially, what this first method of extending your life seems to entail. Is this description of the process for life extension, as it is given above, one a person could accomplish naturally? While this would certainly be an interesting thought. I must say I have grave doubts concerning it.

The Second Method

The second method for the person, who wishes to prolong their life, is to master the art of projecting their non-physical body, along with their entire consciousness, out of their physical body, and into the physical world. Once this art is mastered, the individual must learn to project their non-physical body forcefully into the physical body of another person. Having perfected the art of projection, at the time of their physical death, whether it is voluntary or not, they leave their dying body and project themselves onto another person, displacing the other

IMMORTALITY

persons non-physical body. Naturally they must do so forcefully, even violently if it becomes necessary.

Once in their new body, they must struggle with the consciousness of the one they have invaded, overcome it, and banish it to perdition. The invader takes over the body and mind of the other person, along with the new body's memories and experiences, adding it to their own store of memories, experiences, and the long history of their former life. They then move forward, living their life in their new body as they wish. From the moment they seize control of the body, they have a new vessel of incarnation. Now they live their life in their new body. Their former body, which was entering either natural or violent death at the time, perishes physically as they are occupying the new body.

There apparently is but a short time allowed between the apparent death of the old body and the person's entering into, or connecting to, their new body. I would doubt as much as an hour's lag between these two bodies would be allowed. I would assume that the less time passes, the better it is for the person who wishes to extend their life.

It would seem to me that this method would be the most common, or at least the most possible. It requires no great disadvantages, such as the isolation, great funds, and the honest and reliable associates required to care for the person when they are infants, or otherwise in a state of disability. The other advantage is the transfer of one invisible body to another, along with the replacement of the consciousness, leaves no outward sign. When and if this transfer occurs, there is no external visible trace. Therefore, this transfer is entirely hidden from any possible observation by others, save for a possible change in personality. Such a transfer, if it were accomplished by a discrete and calm personality, would be entirely unsuspected by others.

Naturally, the person forcefully entering into the other person's body must be a fighter, as they must force the consciousness and the non-physical being of the prior resident of the

ON BECOMING IMMORTAL

body into oblivion. Should the prior resident of the body win out in the struggle between them, it is unlikely there would be another chance allowed for the non-physical invader to select a new body as a host. In this case, the hopeful immortal would be the one entering oblivion and perishing. There is a necessity for the hopeful immortal to select the body of a mild and submissive personality to occupy. This would seem to be especially so at their first transfer of bodies.

Two stories follow, concerning the use of this interesting, and to my mind, entirely possible, method of prolonging the existence, if not the life. One of these is told from the point of view of the long-lived one, while the other is told from the point of view of the victim. They are both based on stories I have heard in the course of my life and work. The first I heard from a client, who was a retired military veteran, and a very psychic person indeed. My client told me this was the tale of a medical doctor who treated him for a serious injury while he was in the army. He questioned the doctor in some detail, both consciously and sub-consciously. In his inquiries, he found the doctor to be very open with him concerning his real nature. The doctor had stated quite honestly to my client that no one would ever believe him, to which my client, who did believe him, quickly agreed.

The second story I heard while I was visiting in California in the 1950's. The tale I have written was told me by the man who said it was his life's story. I hardly believed him, considering the nature of the times, but I wrote the essential points of his interesting tale down later in my hotel room. I thought it was certainly a unique story, possibly one suitable for a motion picture. Naturally, I have modified the information given in both of these stories, fleshing out the framework I was told with fiction. I have also changed the names, location, and descriptions of all those involved.

The tale I heard from the man in California originally interested me in beginning to record these adventures of the ex-

IMMORTALITY

ceptionally long-lived. I later learned there are a great many stories of this kind of transfer from the dying body to another younger and more vital one. This exchange seems to regularly occur in India and in other parts of the near east. It seems to be almost a common fete among the higher class of Yogis. As to whether we may accept these stories as being true, I have no idea, although some of the recent experiences of those who have received organ transplants indicate to me the very real possibility of such a thing actually occurring. If so, it seems to me this method is certainly the simplest and most practical means of preserving ones existence, if not the life of their body.

The Third Method

The supposed results of taking the alchemical elixir of life are well enough known that I believe there may actually be something to this. The same details of the process come from widely separated parts of the world. The person so dosed with this elixir becomes insensible, loses their teeth and hair, and must be cared for in every respect, just as a newborn infant. Their need for continual and detailed care continues for some months. The person's skin sloughs off, exposing tender new skin, and their bowels open. They purge themselves so completely, even when they are unconscious, as to often be quite frightening to those who must attend them. The person is to be fed honey water, as much as they can take, and as often as they are awake from their stupor of physical regeneration. It has been suggested that modern intravenous solutions could probably be used to better nourish anyone who might find themselves in this helpless condition.

The person undergoing this change supposedly remains helpless from between six or eight weeks to five or six months. While they are in this rather traumatic state of change, they are for all practical purposes unable to fend for themselves. They require the tender care of one or more attendants, as they have only the physical strength of a baby or infant. They are said to have almost no physical strength at all for the first third of their time of incapacity, when they must be cared for and nurtured as completely as a newborn. As their strength gradually returns, they may be fed fruit juices and broth, as well as honey water. Eventually, as their hair and teeth return, they may slowly begin eating solid food.

In the last third of their period of incapacity, they are able to use a chamber pot or toilet, and to walk about a bit. However, they are still distressingly ill to the eye, and unable to be fully regenerated until the last week or less of their incapacity. Once the malaise of change has passed however, they are said to be stronger and even more vital than they were before this odd adventure. Once this change is complete, the person who has passed through it will never be ill with any disease or illness whatsoever. They cannot be poisoned, and they will maintain their increased strength and vitality for the remainder of their now greatly extended lifetime.

I have heard that the longer the period of physical incapacity the person has suffered, the longer has been their lifespan extended. Of course, as with the other practices supposedly leading to immortality, we have no one stepping forward publicly to say they have experienced this apparent miracle. Instead, we find there are several written remarks and memorials concerning such affairs, but there is no one to say they have actually experienced this transformation. Later I shall give a written testimonial of one who says this has been their own experience, as well as the testimony of someone who says the tale they tell of such a miraculous transformation is true, although they describe it as happening to another.

The reticence of those who may have been transformed by the alchemical fraught is understandable. Should you have been so transformed, would you be willing to step up and so state this to the world? Aside from the fact you would immediately become an object of great curiosity, the skeptics of the world would immediately put the doubt to your words. This would extend to the point you would certainly be the unwelcome recipient not only of those petitioning you for the transformation

IMMORTALITY

themselves, but also of those interested in scorning you as a target for some perverse reason of their own. Moreover, this says nothing concerning those researchers who would be delighted to dissect you while alive, simply to satisfy their own supposed medical, or so called scientific curiosity.

In this regard, I am reminded of Edgar Casey, the famous 'sleeping prophet.' He carried to his grave a scar from a serious knife wound on his hand, inflicted on him by a physician who supposedly wished to 'scientifically' see if Casey was really in a trance.

No, it is quite unlikely any sensible long-lived person will step forward to volunteer they are the recipients of many life times of experience. Instead, it is far more likely they would hide in the shadows, concerned only with their own affairs, moving forward as they desire, to do what they wished in the world. It will be interesting to see if those who are of this nature read any works concerning longevity, or if they actually have any interest in it as a study at all. Having experienced the reality of the process, they are unlikely to wish to deal with the theoretical information concerning it, most especially as the vast majority of this information is written by those who only dream of this miraculous longevity as a fiction, or possibly as a remote possibility.

Two stories of the method of extending life using 'the alchemical elixir of life' are given here. One I heard in a private club, being told by a man who was searching to find the elixir of immortality for himself. A man who claimed it was his own life experience told me the other. I cannot verify either, but I believe they are probably both more or less correct, although I have rather fancifully expanded both of them with fiction, modifying these tales as well. I hid such names, places, and descriptions as I was given, and fleshed out a bit the brief tales I learned from those who told them to me.

I present the following tales as fictions concerning this most interesting subject of human longevity. These stories may

ON BECOMING IMMORTAL

be of some interest to those who enjoy reading of the possibility, or impossibility, of a very long, and hopefully an increasingly prosperous life. They were written based on such facts, as I know, as well as from such tales as others have mentioned to me, and what I have heard at times from various people, in various places. These stories are intended to educate as well as to amuse. The procedures mentioned in this book are certainly not intended to be followed, and obviously, as I myself doubt they might work, they are certainly not to be recommended as useful, much less are they ever to be guaranteed, either by myself or anyone else.

    Naturally, I will state here, of common necessity, all of these stories are fictitious, and are provided only for your entertainment. Any similarity between persons living or dead is entirely accidental, and unintentional. I do sincerely hope you enjoy reading them.

IMMORTALITY

3

Betty and Gloria

My father retired from the army after serving over twenty years as a doctor in the army medical corps. The year he retired, at age fifty, he married my mother, who was thirty years younger than he was. Within a year, she gave him a child, me. By the time I was fifteen, my father was sixty-five or sixty-six, and often said he was interested only in living long enough to see me become a doctor and go into the army, repeating his own life's plan. I really did not know what to think of this, but I supposed it was a plan of sorts. At least becoming a doctor made good sense to me. I knew they made a great deal of money, and my father received a very good pension from his years of army service.

I was a new freshman in high school, and completely embarrassed by the changes puberty was bringing to me. I could hardly talk to other kids, I was shy, and I mumbled instead of speaking, because my voice was cracking and changing. My grades were good, my father's constant pressure and drilling me relentlessly on different subject insured my academic strength. However, I was terribly self-conscious, I had no social life, and was not at all athletic. I was not even a technically savvy computer geek; I was just a total misfit. I did not even play

IMMORTALITY

computer games or do much of anything else. If I was not doing my homework, I stayed in my room, I was actually too embarrassed to even come out of my room and talk to my folks. Talking to other kids my age was almost an impossibility for me.

You would think my parents would know there was something wrong, wouldn't you. Well, they didn't seem to notice. My dad and mom were concerned only with each other, although for mom it seemed she was more concerned that dad die as quickly as possible, so she would have all of the cash and pension benefits she thought she would get from his death to use for herself.

She would even say things to me like, "When your father dies, we can move to a nicer neighborhood." At least she never said such things in front of him, but she would frequently say them to me. She would also smile at me from time to time, as if this were supposed to be our secret conspiracy. Her attitude was not a very good recommendation to me for married life.

Dad ignored all of this. It always seemed to me he idolized mom. He was very affectionate with her, and always very polite to her. He complimented her on every meal she cooked for us, something I often thought was a bit much, but who was I to complain? The food she made was certainly good.

I came home from school on the Friday before Thanksgiving of my freshman year, to find dad meeting me at the door with tears in his eyes and a very sad face. He told me mom had had a heart attack and had died. I was stunned. We held each other and cried like babies for a while. It had happened this morning, she had been in the kitchen and had just fallen over while dad was in the shower. Once Dad found her, he had called the fire department ambulance service, and they tried to revive her. The ambulance took her to the hospital, but it was too late, she was gone. She was at the funeral home now. There would be a quick funeral, sometime before Thanksgiving. What a rotten Thanksgiving this was going to be.

I finally got control of myself, and as I thought dad was in pretty bad shape, we stayed downstairs together. We both

BETTY AND GLORIA

kind of moped around the house a bit. It was weird; as to both of us, it seemed obvious dad should have gone first. He was thirty years older than mom, and I didn't think his health was great, even considering his age. Mom had been only thirty-six, and she had always seemed to be quite healthy to me.

We ordered a pizza, the first time I could remember we had ever done so. Dad and I ate pizza and drank coke in the dining room. We also talked together man to man, another first as far as I was concerned. He was not preaching or pontificating to me either. We were just talking together like two real grown up people. Another big change, I liked it, and I hoped he kept it up.

Once dad retired from the army, he had said he was finished practicing medicine. So, when mom had her heart attack, he did not even have a stethoscope in the house to check her heartbeat with. He blamed himself for that. Later on, he bought some serious first aid and medical stuff for the house. Over time, he taught me how to use it all, saying I should know about such things if I was to become a physician.

Mom's funeral was on the Tuesday before Thanksgiving, and a number of people who had known her turned out for it. I was sad and sulking, and not very good company during the viewing on Monday and the funeral on Tuesday. I had accepted the idea she was dead, but I certainly did not want to believe it. Once I saw the coffin lower into the grave, I knew it really was all over. I cried for a while, Dad and I went home, and while some of the people came over to the house, I just sat around for an hour or so feeling sorry for myself.

Eventually I had some of the cake and stuff, and as people left, I became a little more social. At least I was able to say good-bye to some of the people as they left. Eventually, dad and I were alone with the maid from the catering place who cleaned up and put things away. I was really broken up over mom's death, and I realized it.

Dad and I had another good man-to-man talk, and as he said, it was just going to be the two of us from now on. I told him I would try to stop hiding and start taking some responsibil-

IMMORTALITY

ity for doing things around the house. He said he thought doing so would be good for both of us.

Later we went out for dinner. We decided we would go out for Thanksgiving dinner as well, since neither of us was interested in trying to cook a Thanksgiving meal. It was a dismal Thanksgiving, just as I had thought it would be. One of the hard things for me was when dad gave away the turkey Mom had bought for us. He did give it away on the Wednesday before Thanksgiving when we went out to dinner. He gave it to Mr. Collins, the man who owned the restaurant where we ate. Dad and mom had both known him well.

Mr. Collins expressed his condolences, took the turkey, and left us. I knew we would be eating our Thanksgiving meal at his restaurant, but I hoped we got part of another turkey. I really think we did.

I went back to school on the Monday after Thanksgiving. I was still feeling blue, and I was still painfully shy. I moped my way around the next two days. A number of the kids came up and expressed their condolences to me. I appreciated their thoughts, but each time someone did it, their kind words brought tears to my eyes. Tuesday was better, and things slowly improved for me. By the middle of December, I had pretty much put mom's death behind me, or at least, I thought I had.

Dad and I were getting on a lot better at home now. He began making my breakfast every day, which eventually led to my learning how to cook and later to my making my own breakfast. At least I could make toast, eggs, and sausage, and soon I was making pancakes and some other stuff. By the middle of January, we took turns making breakfast, and dad even said I was becoming a pretty good cook. Now we were talking together more often, and I was actually beginning to come out of my shell and enjoy his company.

Dad usually made dinner, but at least twice a week we would go to the restaurant and eat dinner out. The man who owned the restaurant, Mr. Michael Collins, had been a good friend of both mom and dad, and he was a very pleasant guy. He would come over and talk to us briefly when we were there. He even offered to teach me how to cook, but dad said he would teach me himself. Dad did teach me, and by the time school was out, I was making lunch and dinner for us on the weekends. I was also beginning to be able to make my way through a cookbook without any problem.

    Summer vacation was when dad had always drilled me on the things I would have to know to become a doctor. This year was no exception. I had already learned all of the bones of the body, now he drilled me on the articulations and the places where the muscles connected, their origin and insertion points. By the time I was ready to go back to school, I had learned them all by heart. My school grades had always been good, and in my freshman year, they were still good, despite the huge emotional upset of my mother's death.

    I got off on the right foot in my sophomore year, with Miss Linda Carter who was my English teacher. Everyone in school had nicknamed her 'Wonder Woman,' after the comic strip and movie. She was about my mom's age and a real looker, but she was also a very good teacher. The first week back to school, I was supposed to write a paper describing an emotional experience in my life, so I wrote about my mother's death. Just writing the paper had a kind of purging effect on me. I mean I felt a lot better about myself, and about things in general after I wrote out all of my feelings in the paper.

    Miss Carter called me in and talked to me privately about that paper. Our private discussion led to her kind of opening herself to me, telling me about her own mother's sudden death, which had happened when she was a freshman in college. Afterwards, it was like we had a common bond or something. I mean I liked her as a person, not just as a teacher. It was a kind of neat feeling, although I was not ever sure she really felt the bond as much as I did. Anyway, my liking her class soon led me to doing a lot more, and a lot better, writing. This quickly led to my improving the written assignments for all of my other classes.

IMMORTALITY

    I even had my first date that year. I had been going to the more or less mandatory Friday night school dances, held every other Friday night in the school gym. They were held to supposedly keep us out of trouble. You either attended some of the school dances or you were knocked down a point in your gym class grade. Gym already was my worst grade, so I went to the dances, and I even danced with as many of the girls as I could, just to try to keep my gym grade up. The second dance in September, toward the end of September, I danced with Betty Nelson, and our talking as we danced ended up with her inviting me to take her to the movies. I did. We went to the movies the following Saturday, and considering how shy we both were, we actually had a good time. She was as shy as I was, so after we saw the movies, we had a soda and talked about going to the dances to improve our gym grades. She told me she was not very athletic either, and we both laughed.

    I took her home and met her mother who was divorced. We went out the following week, and she came over to my house and met my dad. Well we decided we liked each other's folks, which led to us admitting to each other we liked each other. Because we could talk to each other, and because we were both painfully shy with other people, we more or less rather quickly drifted into spending a lot of time together. I guess we were going steady, but we never officially said so, we just did not go out with anyone else. I don't think either of us could even manage to ask anyone else for a date.

    My dad was in favor of my dating, he told me it was about time for me to begin socializing with other kids my age. Dad was home almost all of the time, while Betty's mother did not get home until five thirty, so we decided she would come over to my place and we would do our homework together. Once we cleared it with both parents, we came over to my house from school for the first time on a Friday in the middle of October, the week before Halloween. Betty and I were facing a history test, one of the three classes we had together. We were

BETTY AND GLORIA

sitting at the dining room table about five thirty, and asking each other questions out of the book when the doorbell rang.

It was Betty's mother. My dad answered the door. He brought her into the living room, where they began talking.
Well it was six forty five, and we were all finished studying, but my dad and her mom were still talking to each other in the living room. It was getting late, so my dad decided to take us all out to eat.

My dad and Betty's mom ignored Betty and I all through dinner, although Mr. Collins came over to our table and talked to both of them briefly. I guess it was Ok, as Betty and I were talking to each other about school stuff, just as we usually did. Once the dinner was over we went back to my house again, and her mom and my dad kept right on talking to each other in the living room.

Betty and I went up to my room, where I showed her my model airplanes. Later, we watched some television together. About ten thirty we both got tired, so we went to bed. I gave Betty a pair of my pajamas, and she changed in the bathroom while I changed in my room. We both just went to bed and were soon off to sleep.

Naturally, I was curious about her, and I guess she was curious about me, but we did not do anything but go to sleep. I think we were both too shy to even admit we were curious, and I know I was very tired. I think Betty was tired as well.

I went to the bathroom and washed up, came into my room, and dressed. Betty was still asleep in the bed. She looked cute. I went downstairs and made myself some coffee. I cleaned up the dining room of the papers Betty and I had left there last night. Next, I cleaned up the living room, where there were some of my dad's and her mom's clothes. I folded them, setting her mom's clothes neatly on the end of the couch, and hung my dad's in the closet. Afterwards, I went into the kitchen and began making my breakfast.

Betty came down to the kitchen while I was making breakfast. She was still wearing the pajamas I had given her.

IMMORTALITY

They were a little big on her. I told her I thought she looked cute in them. I kissed her, just a peck on the cheek. She blushed, and I put my arms around her and we really kissed. We had kissed passionately before, usually at the end of a date, but somehow it was a little different this time. However, I think we both liked kissing each other with more passion in our kisses. I know she kissed me back as much as I kissed her.

Afterwards we just looked at each other for a few seconds when I suddenly remembered making breakfast and began getting the eggs and the sausage out of the pan and onto my plate. I managed to get Betty a glass of orange juice, and I asked her what she wanted to eat. We got our breakfast stuff together, and soon we were eating breakfast together just as if we did it every day.

Once the dishes were done, we went into the dining room. I had asked Betty if she wanted to get dressed, and she said she wanted to find out what her mom had planned for the day first. I knew my dad was still in bed, and as soon as Betty looked into the living room and saw her mother's clothes, there was no doubt in her mind the two of them were upstairs in bed together. At least she did not blush about it. I told her we could study some more, and she said ok, although she was not very enthusiastic about it. We went over the questions from the history text again, but just looked at each other and gave up the idea of doing any more studying. We ended up sitting in front of the TV in the living room and watching the Saturday morning kiddy shows for a couple of hours.

My dad and her mom finally came downstairs. Dad was dressed, but her mom was only wearing dad's robe. Betty and her mom talked a bit while I set the table and made Dad and Betty's mom some breakfast. Betty went upstairs to dress.

Once dad and Betty's mom were finished eating, they got their clothes from the living room and went back upstairs. I cleared the table and was doing the dishes when Betty came downstairs. She walked over to the sink, picked up a dishtowel, and began drying the dishes. She did not say anything, I looked

BETTY AND GLORIA

at her and smiled, and she smiled back at me. I guess there was really nothing for us to say.

It took a while for dad and Betty's mom to come downstairs again. When they did, they were holding hands and laughing. I was happy for dad. It was the happiest I had seen him in a long time. I knew Betty smiled when she saw how happy her mom was. Once dad and her mom were more or less settled in the living room, her mom said she and Betty were going home. Dad gave her mom a really passionate good-bye kiss, while Betty and I gave each other a considerably less passionate one. I think we were both concerned about our parents. Dad was sixty-seven, and her mom was only thirty-three, which was even younger than my mom had been. The age disparity did not seem to worry either of them. It looked to me like the two of them were already very much in love.

Once Betty and her mom left, dad went back upstairs. He was whistling. Wow, that was a real change. I was glad he was so happy. I finished cleaning the kitchen and the dining room, and took what few things I had laying around up to my bedroom. Personally, I thought my going out with Betty had just been ended, but I was not sure. I wanted to talk to dad about things, but he was busying himself in his bedroom, and soon he left the house.

I really wanted to talk to dad and find out what was going on. I also wanted to ask his advice about Betty. Unfortunately, he was not here. I did some housework, then settled on watching TV in the living room for a while, although I thought it was a very poor substitute for talking to dad. After a while I went up to my bedroom, got into my pajamas, and took a nap. I think I was actually more bored than tired, but I slept soundly anyway.

It was after three in the afternoon when I finally woke up. Betty was standing right by the side of my bed, smiling down at me. She had kissed me awake and now was saying something to me about how the girl was supposed to be the sleeping beauty, while the guy was supposed to be the one to

IMMORTALITY

kiss her awake. I finally woke up enough to reach up and put my arm around her. She bent down over me and kissed me again. This time we kissed passionately, no tongue, but still it was a passionate kiss for us. I let go of her and got out of bed, sitting on the side of the bed.

I told her, "I have to go the bathroom." I blushed, I was embarrassed, and I hoped she would not say anything. Waking up like that was the most embarrassing thing I had ever had happen to me in my life. I could feel myself blush as I stood up and walked into the bathroom.

I had noticed Betty had changed clothes, but I had no idea what else was going on with her and her mother. I did know it was way past lunchtime, and I wondered if she had eaten. When I got back into my bedroom, I asked her if she had eaten lunch. She said she and her mom had both had lunch. I noticed there was a suitcase sitting next to my clothes closet. I looked from it to her, and she blushed. All right, I guess it meant she was moving in with me. Ok with me, as far as I was concerned. At least I guessed it was going to be Ok. I assumed it meant her mom was going to be moving in with dad. Ok, this was something new. What did all this mean? I had no idea.

What I wanted to do now was to get dressed. I had put my pajamas on for my nap, just as I usually did. I wondered if I could get dressed with Betty in my room watching me. I only hesitated a second, and decided I would try it. I took off my pajama top and when I did, she handed me my t-shirt. Ok, we were off to a good start. I put it on, reached over to the pile of clothes, and got my shorts. I turned away from her, dropped my pajama bottoms, and put my shorts on. Well then, putting my pants and shirt on was no problem at all. I thought to myself this living together stuff might just work out after all.

Once I had my shoes and socks on we went downstairs. My dad and her mom were in the kitchen, where her mom was making a cake. Dad looked at me with a big grin and told me Gloria and Betty would be staying with us over the weekend. He added that Betty would go to school with me on Monday, and come home with me, staying with us until Gloria got home from work.

Once he told us, Betty's mom, (Gloria – It had to be her mom's name) turned to us and gave us all a big smile. I just nodded. Ok, this was more or less what I thought had happened. I looked at Betty. She was smiling as well. I guessed everyone approves of this arrangement. Well then, so do I. Betty got me a cup of coffee, and she and I sat down at the kitchen table with dad. Gloria had put the batter in the cake pans, and was bouncing out the air bubbles. She put the cake pans in the oven, set the timer, and turned to dad.

She said, "Half hour to play," and sat on dad's lap.

He just grinned. I wondered if it was my clue to leave the room, Betty was staying, so I guessed it was Ok if I stayed. They kissed, both of them using a lot of tongue. Their kissing was embarrassing me. I asked Betty if she wanted to go into the living room and watch TV. We did, but I kind of got the idea she would rather have stayed and watched my dad and her mom make out. I knew my dad and her mom making out embarrassed me, but I had no idea what I could do about it.

We watched TV for a while, sitting together on the couch, and holding hands on and off. I was comfortable being with her, but I had no real idea what I was expected to do next. I mean how do you go from the stage of closed mouth kissing to the great-unknown mystery of actually having sex with a girl. I was sure Betty was ready for me to do whatever I wanted to do with her. At least I thought she was, but I really did not know what I wanted to do, or how to do it. I was very nervous and uncertain about just what I was expected to do next. I was not even sure just how far, or how fast, I wanted to go with her. Naturally, as I usually did when I was uncertain, I just hid inside myself and avoided the issue completely.

Dad and Gloria certainly were not the least bit unsure of themselves. We couldn't see them from where we were sitting, but we could both hear them. They were making a lot of happy moans, sighs, and squeals. In the midst of one of them, Betty

IMMORTALITY

turned to me and we both blushed. I think her blush told me she was as unsure about what to do as I was. Somehow, the observation that she was equally uncertain about what to do made me feel a little better.

After the cake came out of the oven, Dad and Gloria went upstairs to the bedroom. Betty and I watched TV sitting on the couch with our arms around each other. We had mutually agreed we would probably be going out to eat tonight. I was not hungry, but I thought Betty might be. She said she wasn't hungry. Suddenly she leaned right into me and kissed me.

The kiss started out as a normal kiss, but it became an open mouth kiss almost right away, and it quickly went further. Betty put her hand on the back of my head and drew me into her, as her tongue cleaned my teeth. I responded, doing much the same thing, and soon we were in the most passionate kiss of my life. I had an arm around her shoulder, and she had her hand behind my head. With our tongues in each other's mouth, she put my other hand on her breast. I knew I was in heat, but I was still unsure of what to do. I caressed the side of her breast gently, and then decided to just go for it. I put my hand down to the bottom of her sweater, and pushed it up. In an instant, my hand was on her bare breast. Never having had my hand anywhere near a girl's breast before, I had not realized she was not wearing a brassiere. She sighed, and put her hand over mine, not retraining me, but encouraging me on. I was amazed by how soft her breast was.

She moved her hand and began stroking my head and rubbing my back at the same time. I felt her nipple, and it seemed to be hard. I knew my cock certainly was. It was caught in my underpants and it was definitely uncomfortable. I broke away from her and stood up, as I had to adjust myself in my pants. As soon as I stood, Betty took my hand and led me right upstairs to my bedroom. We undressed each other in a maze of kisses and caresses, and soon we were in bed together. Once in bed, I discovered Mother Nature had provided instincts to guide us further along in getting together sexually. We gently made love, afterwards resting in each other's arms, just cuddling and kissing each other for quite some time.

I discovered making love to a girl was very pleasurable. It was even more pleasurable than I had imagined it could be, and frankly, I had imagined doing it quite a lot. Holding, kissing and caressing Betty was the most wonderful thing in the world to me. Her body was so soft and nice it was positively amazing. I decided I loved her. She was so responsive to me I was simply enthralled by it.

Just before we were ready to make love again, I told her we shouldn't as she might become pregnant. She smiled and told me she was on the pill. She added she had been on the pill since she was thirteen to keep her from getting acne. I briefly wondered if it was the same pill, but I did not say anything to her. I really just wanted to make love to her again. I did. We both decided we truly enjoyed doing it with each other.

With that, we began what I later called the weekends of passion. In mid December, my dad and Gloria were married, which meant Betty permanently moved in with us. Gloria sold her house, and she and dad were as happy as two bugs in a rug, so to speak.

So were Betty and I. We had become friends before we began having sex, and we really enjoyed each other's company. We explored each other sexually as much as possible, and I think we did everything two people could possibly do with each other. At least we did everything we could think of. We were amazingly open with each other, both verbally and sexually, especially considering we were so shy with everyone else.

We set up a bedroom for Betty, but she was actually sleeping with me every night. Sleeping with her was interesting, as I am reasonably certain I was the only guy in my high school that was having sex every day. Betty and I made love every morning and every night, as well as most days when we came home from school. It was as if we really wanted to just feast on each other sexually. We did everything sexual with each other we could dream of doing. I thought being with her every day

IMMORTALITY

was just positively wonderful. Best yet, was that our relationship was so wonderful for both of us. She enjoyed it as much as I did. We wallowed in both conversations and the flesh, never denying each other anything.

Naturally, I never told anyone we were having sex, and neither did she. We knew it would have caused a huge hassle in school. On the other hand, we were together as much as we could be in school. I guess you could say we were pretty much clones in school, holding hands as much as possible. I thought most of our fellow students just thought we were going steady. Well, I guess we actually were.

During my summer vacation, dad and I went over the names and functions of all of the muscles in the human body, and reviewed everything I had learned so far. I got all the muscles down pat as well. I entered my junior year with a 3.89 average, which was good if I say so myself. Betty had about the same; she was planning to go on to college as well.

I was almost used to having her in bed with me, and while I realized how lucky I was, I realized I was becoming accustomed to having her in bed with me now. On the other hand, we certainly did get along well. We never argued or quarreled, and we were always considerate of each other. Dad and Gloria were the same. The four of us made an interesting set. On weekends, the four of us went out to dinner together every Saturday night. Mr. Collins would come over to our table and say hello, and usually talk for a while. He was soon as friendly with Gloria as he had been with mom, when we came here with her and dad.

One interesting thing was, Gloria never seemed to be looking forward to dad dying like mom had been. She always treated him really well, like Betty treated me. I guess dad and I were both very happy with the two women we had with us. I knew I was certainly happy with Betty.

In my junior year, we had to make application for scholarships so we did. We had already decided we would only go to school together. We wanted to go to the state university, which had a branch in town. I would try to go to the state University Medical School, which was only about thirty miles away. Like I said, it was a plan. I got an Army ROTC scholarship to the state university, which would even pay my way through medical school if I maintained a 3.8 average in pre med. Betty got a regular scholarship, with four years of paid education. It was a good deal for both of us. As a part of my scholarship, I was obliged to spend at least seven years in the Army once I finished medical school. Doing so was no big thing to me, as I intended to make a career out of the army anyway.

    To enhance my army career, I joined the Army Reserve. I was assigned to a Reserve Evacuation Hospital as an orderly. Because of all the things I had studied with dad, when I went thorough medical orderly training the summer between my junior and senior year, I graduated at the top of my class and was promoted to corporal.

    My senior year in high school went by rapidly. I had my future all planned out for the next sixteen years. The officer who had set up my scholarship had explained all of the details to me. I would be getting a commission once I graduated from pre med, and would be going to medical school as a second lieutenant. I would be paid for going to school, as well as getting a free education. It was a very good deal for me, as far as I was concerned.

    Betty and I decided we could be married after we graduated from college. We were both looking forward to it.

    The scholarship officer said I would have four years of medical school followed by a year of internship at an army hospital. Then I would begin serving my seven years of required service, so at the end of the seven years I would actually have twelve years of active service plus five years of reserve service as an enlisted man. I would have seventeen years of service, meaning I would only have three years more to serve before I retired with a reserve pension, or eight years to retire with a much larger active duty pension. I would actually be able to retire at any time between age thirty seven and forty two if I was

IMMORTALITY

playing my cards right. Dad said it was a much better deal than he had, as he had not been able to attend medical school as an officer on active duty. My advantage was the Army really needed some career medical officers now.

Things went along pretty much right on schedule. I graduated from medical school, and my father, who was now seventy-eight years old, welcomed me home. I was due to report to the Walter Reed Army Hospital to begin my internship in thirty days.
She and her mother Gloria went out to go clothes shopping, as she and I had almost been living out of a suitcase while I was in medical school. We had been holding down our expenses, so we could afford the move to the Army Hospital where I would serve my internship.
Dad and I were having celebratory beer on the front porch. He went in the house, returning in a short while and handing me another beer. A police car drove up and parked in front of our house about a half hour later. The officer came up on the porch and told us Gloria and Betty had both been killed in an automobile accident. Naturally, we were both shocked.
To my great surprise, Dad coughed, sputtered, and just fell over. His beer bottle rolled to the edge of the porch and fell off the porch, tight into the flowerbed below. The officer and I both tried to help him sit up, but I could feel he was already gone. My first thought was, 'the shock of Gloria's death killed him.'
Suddenly, something very strange began happening to me. It was as if dad was entering into me, not coming in nicely, as I would think spirit possessions I had read about might happen. He was entering me almost viciously. He was charging into me, as if he was going to take me over. He was just kind of pushing the me that I believed I was aside, and starting to take over both my body and my mind. That part of me was just folding up in fear. I knew I was reacting to this physically in some

way. However, I had no real idea what was actually happening to me.

The police officer had gone back to his car to call for an ambulance for dad. When he returned to the porch, he saw I was sitting somewhat dazed, or in shock, I guess, in the chair. I heard him say he would go in the house and get me a drink of water. I heard myself faintly reply I would be ok. The difference was, somehow I knew dad had made my body say those words. I was sitting there wondering just what had happened to me, and actually being rather fearful of what was happening, as it seemed I had no control at all over it.

Nevertheless, I somehow knew dad was taking over my body and mind. It was a very weird feeling, and it really scared me. On the other hand, I could feel I was fading away, like I was leaving my body, and just giving it over to him.

As dad was taking me over, some of his memories came passing through my mind. Suddenly I somehow knew things. Dad had killed Gloria and Betty for their insurance money, as well as to get them out of his way. I suddenly realized he had killed my mom as well. He knew very well she was looking forward to his dying. He had deliberately killed her somehow, to shut her up, as well as to collect on her life insurance, which I suddenly learned had been substantial. For some reason, he had wanted me to finish medical school before he took me over. I could feel the me I had thought I was shrinking into nothing, as what dad was expanded the him inside me. I suppose this is an odd way to put it, but I could not think of any other way to phrase what was happening. He was quickly filling up all of the body and mind I had formerly thought had been mine. He was filling me with himself.

Now that I had graduated from medical school, and he had killed off Betty and Gloria, he could move himself completely into me. He no longer needed his old body. Now he would possess my considerably younger body as his own.

I was fading away, but as I did, I faintly saw battlefields from old wars. I saw shadowed scenes of people dying and others of people starving. I thought I saw people from ancient times and the middle ages. I saw wars, plagues, and the ugly side of the ancient medical profession, which had treated all of these horrors. There were faint images of piles of amputated limbs, and people doing amputations without anesthetic. People were screaming, while others, nearly dead, were dying in great pain. It was horrible, and I knew it was all from the memories of dad's prior lives leaking into my mind.

    Dad was always the savior, the doctor who took care of the injured, the sick, and the wounded. As he did, he sucked the life force out of the dying. People loved him, and he fed on their love and affection, but he would take their life force away from them as well. He would just suck it out of them whenever he wanted to do so. He could control them as if they were puppets on strings. I realized he had made Gloria fall in love with him as soon as she met him. He had also made Gloria think Betty and I getting together sexually as high school sophomores was really a good thing for her, as well as for me.

    My father was pulling the strings. I felt my body sobbing and I knew dad was making my body cry. I really just wanted to scream. I could feel my dad inside me, calmly looking at me, smiling, and telling me to just accept what was happening to me, as I had no choice, and no control at all over the process. He told me somehow he had done this dozens, if not scores of times before, and he would do it dozens and scores of times again. He told me I would soon be gone, and he would be running what had once been me, with all of my memories and all of my knowledge just being added to all of his own. At least he was not laughing at me. He was just calmly explaining things to me, as what I had always thought I was, gradually faded away into nothing at all.

    The people from the fire department ambulance came and took my dad and I to the hospital. I could hear my dad using my body to tell them he would be all right once he had slept. The idea of sleep terrorized me. Somehow, I knew once my body was asleep, I would be gone forever, and dad would be in charge of my body and mind for as long as my body was alive. They put me on a bed in the emergency room and gave me a sedative. As I went off, unwillingly, to sleep, I could hear my dad telling me Betty and Gloria had been very good for us while they lasted. He seemed to think this was some kind of a consolation for me.

My last memory as I drifted off to sleep was that the body I had once had used was softly crying, as what I had once thought I had been completely perished. Only my father remained inside my body now.

~-~

The new intern at Walter Reed was obviously one of those rare men who were born to be a physician. He had a great bedside manner, and was more than competent as a diagnostician. Major Jeffries, who was in charge of the interns, wrote up a glowing recommendation for the man. When the young physician mentioned he would like to become a surgeon, Major Jeffries approved this as well. Everyone in the hospital thought he was a perfect physician, and believed he would make a truly great surgeon. He was promoted to Captain during the final year of his residency. He was always highly commended by all who knew him, not only for his medical skill, but also for his unusually deep grasp of the history of military medicine. He told people the history of military medicine had been his hobby when he was in high school. He assured everyone who asked that he had always wanted to become a doctor.

IMMORTALITY

Varmus

I sit alone in this room, this single room occupancy, which I have designated as my place to die this time. I look out the window, waiting, but not for anything happening outside of me. I am waiting to die, so I can be reborn. All of this will happen inside of me. It has happened many times before, and is a quite familiar process to me now.

Painful yes, but it is only very briefly painful, and only when I stop my heart. The pain is necessary, as no body can live forever, and each must eventually die in its turn, no matter how long it may live. As I look out the window, I hope to see a body I can inhabit when I die. I am looking for a body in the prime of health, about twenty-four or five, well featured, strong, intelligent, and athletic. I'm asking for a lot from my fourth floor single room. This neighborhood does not draw many such excellent people to it. I may have to ride on one of those passing below me until I can find someone suitable to inhabit. I have done that before as well. At my age, there is little in my existence I do not find to be a repetition. However, I prefer routine, I have always made it a point not to seek novelty.

Although as I sit in this chair waiting for the time for my body to die, I am very aware I carry in my mind the long series

IMMORTALITY

of memories of my past lives. My rent is paid until the end of next month, I am always paid at least a month in advance, and I always tell the man in charge my young nephew is coming to see me. This is to give me at least two weeks to take command of my new body. Gaining full command of the new body is something I have learned I must allow for. Some bodies, but only a very few, are rebellious at discovering a change of ownership is occurring within them. However, I always win. I do not ever fight fair, especially when I am taking possession of a new body I particularly want.

My mind reaches back to the beginning, and by happening, I know the time for my body's death approaches quickly. The end always starts in this way. I have given strict orders for the building staff not to disturb me. I am ready. I sigh and relax, determined to ride a body until I can find one I wish to inhabit. It will not take me long. I know what I want, and I am reasonably sure where I can find one.

I was born on a breeding farm, where slaves were raised for sale. I have no idea who my parents were, as I was put to a wet nurse so my mother could be bred again. When I was quite young, I was selected to become a porter, one who carries heavy goods. I was trained to lift loads and move things. My body was built large and my frame heavy, I was soon as strong as anyone was then, and much stronger than most. When I was fourteen or fifteen, possibly younger, I was sold as a porter along with a number of others. We went to a slave buyer for the legion of Cedilla. He was leading an expedition south. I had no idea where south was. I thought south was another farm, or possibly a city.

I found I was to carry a load of goods over half my weight, walking along behind the servant of an officer in the legion named Marcus. I set the burden down when we rested, and his servant got things from the load Marcus wanted. I was the invisible one, the unknown porter who no one noticed. My invisibility was fine with me. I have ever since preferred to remain invisible and unnoticed to other people.

VARMUS

We walked for many days, and we took to a ship for many more days. Finally, we got off the ship at a place where it was very hot. I stayed off with the baggage train while the legion fought briefly. We began walking south again. We walked over sand and through rocky land. I ate, I drank water, and I walked. We stopped at one place where the legion fought, and I again stayed with the baggage train. The legion reformed and we walked some more. I was content, as this was the life for which I had been born. I was certain this was all I would ever know of life. I had been born for this work.

The storm came upon us suddenly. It came when we were all in the midst of a large field of sand, as big as any field I had ever seen. I hid behind my load, putting it between the wind and myself. The wind blew for three days, piling sand everywhere. You could hardly see or even breathe for the sand blowing. The man who was the servant of Marcus either died or ran away, I did not care which. He left his water bladders, so I took them. The second day of the windstorm, I emptied the first bladder. I put it back where I had found it, although there was just sand there now. His goods were all covered with sand.

I constantly had to lift my load from the sand and reposition both it and myself. I did not sleep well for those three days, as the sand quickly covered those who slept. I had to relocate my load every short while. I never let my load or I become more than a third of my half height covered with sand. By the middle of the fourth day, the wind died completely, just as if it had never been. I had just emptied the second water bladder. I was delirious, and I saw visions. My eyes would not focus. I pulled a covering from my load and covered myself with it. I slept, and woke when it grew cold. It was night. A clear night, the stars were bright.

I was hungry, and I was thirsty. There was nothing but hard salt biscuits in the load. I was not supposed to eat those biscuits. They belonged to Marcus. However, I could not see Marcus or anyone else. I took one of the biscuits and ate it. I looked around, but I could not find anyone within my sight.

IMMORTALITY

There was no one left of the legion. There was nothing but sand as far as I could see.

I slept again, but I was thirsty. In the morning, I woke with the sun as I usually did. I still could not see anyone. I stood and looked all around myself. There was nothing but sand where we had been marching. I wondered if I was the only one left alive. How could such a thing be? I stood and continued walking, with my load on my back. It was what I had been born to do. I knew nothing else. I walked for some time. Eventually, in the distance, I saw some horses.

The horses were coming toward me. As they came closer, I saw there were people riding on them. Soon they were near me. They stopped looking at me, I asked for water, pointing a finger to my mouth. They gave me some water to drink. One of them took my load and unpacked it, examining it closely. They talked among themselves in a language I did not know. One of the men handed me the biscuits, there were five of them left. He signed me I could eat them, and I ate two of them. They talked among themselves as I ate, but they gave me more water, this time a whole bladder full. I drank a lot of the water and my stomach revolted. I was sick, and ashamed of myself. One of the men told me with signs to eat another biscuit, and I did. I felt a bit better. He gave me something to drink, not water, but good tasting. I found my stomach quieted. They gave me back my load, and seemed to be asking me where I was going. I had no answerer to the question. I was just going on, carrying my load. Carrying my load was what I did. It was all I did. They smiled, being quite friendly toward me.

They let me join them, my load was put on one of the horses, and soon we were at their city of tents. I was put in a tent with another man, but he could not speak my language. I slept, and they fed me there for three or four days.

Eventually a man who could speak my language came to talk to me. He asked me how I had happened to be in the midst of the sand. I told him about the legion, the marching, and the sand blowing all over us for three days. He took it all down, writing on a parchment. I had seen writing before, but not very often. I had never seen anyone write as fast as he did. Of course, I could not read any of it. The man left me once I had told him my story.

Later the man who had first signed to me came and gave me a large piece of meat to eat. He was smiling. I had only had meat to eat on a rare feast day before. It was the first time in my life I had had a piece of meat this big to eat. I ate it slowly, savoring it. He also gave me soft cakes, water, and some of the sweet drink of not water.

The man who had spoken to me in my language came and said they were giving me a feast because what I had told them had made them very happy. He added I could stay with them now, as the entire legion had been covered with the sandstorm, and they believed all of the men had perished. I told him I would be pleased to stay with them, but I had no idea about what I could do, as I was only a porter. He smiled, and said first I had to learn to talk with them. I eagerly told him I would like to learn to talk to them.

I slept in the tent with the man who did not speak my language, but the next day they moved me to another smaller tent, where I was to spend time with another man. He signed and made noises at me. Soon I got the idea he was teaching me their language. It took me a great deal of time, but I finally learned to speak their language and to understand them. All this time, I spent all day with the man, and he showed me how to speak their language by walking me around and pointing things out to me, repeating their name, until I understood the name and could say the word properly. The tent city had to move, so it went off, traveling for three days, where it went into a city.

There the man who spoke my language came to me again, and he told me, this time in his language, the people wished to sell me to pay for my keep while I was with them. Naturally, I thought this was fair, as they had fed me well, and had taken good care of me. I told him I had no objections to their selling me in the slave market. He nodded and said it was

IMMORTALITY

good. Then he took me to a man who he said was the chamberlain of the ruler of the city in which we were now located.

The chamberlain waited on the monarch, who it seems, had bought me from the people of the tents. In a short time, I was brought before the monarch, and he asked me what I did best. I told him I was a porter and carried things for people. He smiled and assigned me to an old man. He told the old man I could carry him around wherever he wanted to go. I told him I would carry him, and I went over to stand next to the man. When the audience with the monarch was over, the old man had me kneel down so he could climb on my shoulders. He told me where to carry him. I took him to his house, which was in the monarch's building, called the palace.

There he had me kneel again, so he could get off my back. The old man was one of the monarchs' physicians. He had me undress, and had me bathe. He examined me more thoroughly than I had been examined by anyone before. He told me I was a good subject, and began to talk to me.

"What is your name?"

"Porter."

"No, Porter is what you do, what is it people call you?"

"Porter. They never call me anything but Porter."

"Well porter will not do at all, you must have a name. Let me see, you were found on the western edge by the sea, so we shall have call you something having to do with being lost near the seashore. In addition, it should be at least close to your native language, so it sounds like it was your original name.

The old man went to the shelves where he had any number of scrolls. He selected one, and read in it. He finally found a name for me. It was Varmus, which is the name I have used for myself ever since. I have no idea how he selected it. He seemed to think it was a humorous name, but his jest did not bother me, I now had a name. I was no longer just another nameless slave. Somehow, having my own name made a big difference to me.

VARMUS

The old man told me he was a physician in charge of caring for the temple servants, as well as the monarch. The he told me the temple servants were of two kinds, those who lived and died, and those who lived forever. I looked oddly at him when he spoke, he nodded, all full of enthusiasm. He said he was training a new group of temple servants to live forever, as they had all just taken new bodies. He wanted me to carry him to the temple. Naturally, I agreed to do so. I really was beginning to think he was insane, although I knew he could not hurt me, I was far stronger than he was.

The old man got on my back and we went to the Temple, which was a large building almost in the center of the city. He had me take him to a certain room, and set him down. We waited, and in a short time, several people came in to sit on the floor near us. He lectured them on the process of getting themselves out of their bodies and attaching themselves to another body. He talked about it for some time, and he answered their questions. It was interesting, but I did not understand very much of it. When the lecture was over, I carried him back to his house, and we had our lunch. I must say he ate well, having meat at every meal. As he shared all of his meals with me, I also ate very well the whole time I was with him.

As we had our lunch, he continued telling me how you got all of yourself out of your old body when it died, and put all of yourself into another new body. He said he would be giving several more talks to those people at the Temple, and I told him I would carry him there and back. I do not think he believed I was interested in what he said about living forever, but I was. Some part of me liked the idea. I wondered if I could do the trick when it was time for me to die. I decided I would try to learn how to do it.

Over the next month or so, I heard all of his lectures, and carried the old man all over the city. He had given the people he was talking to about living forever some exercises. I did them myself, practicing them at night when I was supposed to be sleeping. I think I did them correctly, as events later proved I

IMMORTALITY

had. I never asked him about the exercises, nor did I ever even seem to be curious about living forever. I was afraid if I showed any interest, he would do something to put an end to his talking to me about it.

I realized after my first day or so with him, despite his talking to me, he considered me a dumb brute with no mind. His opinion did not surprise me, most people thought of me as having no mind. People's indifference did not trouble me at all, as his thinking of me as being a dumb brute way allowed him to talk to me about living forever and say any number of other things I found interesting.

I was not popular in the palace, but I was not shunned or despised either. Mostly, I was just ignored. I accepted it, as it had always been so with me. I carried the old man, and paid attention to things, but I never let anyone learn I knew anything at all of what they spoke. By playing dumb, I managed to overhear some very interesting conversations. I also learned a great deal about how things were done in the city, as well as much about how things were done in the outside world. I continued to practice the exercises at night, and became, at least to my own mind, quite proficient at them.

I had come to the city when I thought I was perhaps fifteen or sixteen years old. The old man died after I had been with him about five or six years. Therefore, I thought I was about twenty years old when he died. One of the people from the temple came to me, told me the old man had died and led me away. I was taken to the temple and put with their other slaves. They used me as brute labor there, lifting heavy things and moving things as I was directed to do. I worked there for many years. I believe I worked there for almost forty years, I do not know. I ate well, I worked hard, and I slept well. That was my life.

All that time I remained conscious of what I had leaned about living forever. I also kept right on practicing the exercises, as I had no idea when I would have them perfected. In the fullness of time, I realized death was not so far away from me. One day I was so ill that I could not get out of my bed. I lay back in the bed. One of my roommates noticed I was ill, and in a bad way.

Someone summoned one of the temple attendants. I saw the attendant enter with one of the young physicians. I knew neither of them was one of those who lived forever. I willed myself to die just as the young physician bent over me. I left my body and attached myself to him. I knew I had perfected the exercises, as at night, when the physician slept I entered into him and became him. I entered fully into his body, occupying it for myself. The part of him he thought about as himself was pushed aside, it either left or it perished, I know not which, but I knew it was gone. What I was now controlled his conscious mind, his memories, and all of his skills. All of the experiences he had had so far in his life were now mine. I had died physically in my old body, but the person who had been the physician had actually been the one who had perished.

I had now become a physician attached to the temple. From being an uneducated porter, I was now an educated physician. I took his memories and experiences into myself greedily. I was happy the trick the old man had taught me had worked. Now I knew that I would live another life.

The following day the physician missed work, as he told the attendants he was ill. However, by next sunrise, I had completely occupied his body and mind, and made all of what had ben his, my own. I went out into the day a confident, although quite young, temple physician. It seemed to me no one knew the difference. If anyone noticed any change, they said nothing about it to me or to anyone else. I truly believe no one noticed anything different at all. However, the though that someone might notice there had been a change in the young physician haunted me for quite some time.

I treated the sick as an employee of the temple. I was well paid, and I had a female slave to care for me. I attended classes in healing as well as attending many of the rituals held in the temple. I was respectful to everyone, and obsequious only to the high priest of the temple. The young physician had behaved

IMMORTALITY

in this way previously, so I continued to behave in this way. On the other hand, I found this new body too frail for my liking. I was used to being physically powerful, so I began exercising, and engaging in active physical sports. Exercising was easy, as was joining into the group of men who passed a heavy ball around their circle in the courtyard of the temple every day. The men were glad to have me join their sport. Soon I was made a member of the green team, and accepted by all of them.

No matter how much I exercised, I would never have the powerful body of a porter. However, I did not need a powerful body either. I was being compensated to use my head rather than my muscle. Using my mind was a very new idea to me. As having been a porter, I found it interesting to watch myself work as a physician.

I had told people I wanted to develop myself physically to increase my stamina, saying a strong body was more resistant to illness than a weak one. The other men in the temple certainly agreed with this. Quite soon, I was also doing the exercises to leave my body at night. Between those and my physical exercises to develop my body during the day, I was quickly in very good physical condition. The dual exercise regime was quite beneficial for me. Within three years, I was sure my body had attained the maximum strength and stamina I could expect to get from it. I was also confident I could go into another body when I died.

As a physician, I was expected to travel around perfecting myself in my craft until I had forty years, at which time I would be expected to settle down and teach my trade to others. Things were done in particular way then, and I had no quarrel with the system. I wanted to leave the temple area and the city anyway, as I still had what I later discovered to be an unreasonable fear that someone would notice I was just the former porter, who had once carried around one of the monarch's physicians.

As I exercised and built myself up, I slowly learned many people who had learned this technique of immortality died through accidents and injuries, either before they could leave their bodies, or shortly afterwards. Thus, even among those living in the protected influence of the temple, the small number of immortals actually decreased slightly each year or so. The old physician I had carried about had not managed to enter properly and fully into a body before the body he had entered into had been kicked by a horse. The kick had placed his body into a coma, and the old physician had passed on in the comatose state. From being an immortal, he was now as dead as any other ordinary man who had ever died with their body.

    I became more aware of those who I knew were the immortals of the temple. I now observed them with the eye of the physician I had become. The bodies they had chosen were not all suited to a vigorous and healthy life. I decided I would have no problem, with these supposed immortals, as in time I was sure they would all die off. I was determined I would not. I began assessing, with the new mind of the physician I had become, what kind of body I should have to enter into, to be sure of a long, healthy, and vital life. I also carefully assessed what kind of personality I could easily overcome when I took possession of the new body. I had been fortunate this time, but life provided no guarantees. I would have to be observant and careful the next time I took a body.

    Meanwhile, I had been at the temple for five years and it was time for me to leave, traveling on to finding more to learn of the physician's arts. I procured horses, and with my slave girl, I set out with a caravan headed for the north. The caravan was accompanied by a number of guards, and the master of the caravan welcomed the services of a physician on his journey. I slowly traveled for three weeks, and entered a city to the north I thought I remembered as the place where the legion had set out from so many years ago. I was likely wrong in my estimation, but it made no difference to me. It was a large city for the times, and I could live here comfortably.

    I left the caravan and registered with the physician's guild of the city. I managed to obtain a small assignment as a physician at the port, charged with inspecting slaves coming into the

IMMORTALITY

city to be sold. It was not a very profitable assignment, and it was mine because the aging man who had held it for many years had recently died. However, it was a worthwhile task to my eyes, as it gave me some income, and provided for me otherwise. Many of the other physicians of the city came to observe me examine the slaves. It was only a day or so after I had been so closely observed by some of them, they decided I was a true physician, and admitted me completely to their company. Their acceptance allowed me the real companionship of my peers. I was certainly a willing student, listening respectfully to all of them.

    I remained in the city for another five years and headed off for the Ionian Isles, where one of the leading physicians of the time lived. I was determined to study with him, but I was barely able to meet the aged man before he took ill and died. However, I joined his company, and learned a great deal from his students, who were most willing to share what they had learned from him. I only remained there for three years. I headed east to the shore of the Mediterranean, where I joined the famous medical clinic of Aleppo. The members of the clinic had invited me to join them. My body was near forty years old, now, so I decided to remain here and learn what I could while I attempted to make plans for my future existence. It was a good plan. I married well, buried my slave girl when she died, and had three children by my wife. I became one of the leading physicians of the city of Aleppo, and in time, people of the city respected me as a leader of the physicians. I died and passed into the body of a young military officer who happened to be passing by my window when I expired. This experience got me into attempting to die while sitting at a window. I have actually been quite successful at doing this over the years.

    My new body was of a strong handsome brute of a man. Actually, he reminded me of myself in my years as a porter. On the other hand, I was not interested in dieing in the military, much less perishing in any kind of war. I became a deserter, and soon a criminal, stealing from both the weak and the rich. I was a skilful and vicious footpad, in an era when it was a common and very violent trade.

My new body had received all kinds of fighting training. It even bore several scars to show it had been involved in a real war or two. Being a trained soldier, I was well equipped to be a far fiercer fighter than the average footpad. I made my way south, doubled back and came north, avoiding Aleppo completely. By the time I arrived at Corinth, I had a decent collection of funds; three horses, a slave girl, and no one knew who I was. I settled there for a time, living in idle luxury as I prepared myself for my next existence. I had decided I wished to become a member of the very wealthy idle rich for a time. My military body had a disease, something while not at all obvious, certainly was fatal.

I sat at a window as I degenerated, becoming more helpless by the day, until I died. I immediately landed on the back of a passerby and forced him to go to the richest quarter of the city, where I found the man I wished to inhabit, within the hour. I was on him in an instant, and I began settling into him immediately, as I needed the energy. He was invested in disporting himself, dedicating his life to ruining himself with drink and women.

Once I had his body completely under my control, I put a stop to his dissipation and drinking. I quickly began building his body into something with more muscles than flab. His family was delighted he had 'seen the light,' and had reformed himself. I was delighted he was becoming a good vehicle for me to use. Within a year, he was as good a vehicle for me as any other body I had ever inhabited.

I found to my surprise the idle rich were as circumscribed by rules and restrictions as any common person. I had meetings to attend, plans to make and investments to consider. Pleasure was one thing I had in excess, but with pleasure, came responsibility. My life was hardly free. Once my 'father' died and I became the 'man of the house,' my responsibilities further increased. I thought about this and decided I had almost been

IMMORTALITY

better off as a porter. I had children by my three wives, and several concubines. I picked one of the boys to be my heir. By selecting the most serious, I believed I was passing on the family funds. I grew old and again sat at a window awaiting my death.

It came in time, and I was soon in another body, this one a merchant, a dealer in leather hides. He was far more effective than the rich man had been. I lived a life with him, and went overseas on a trading voyage, where I died in a new land. I found a new body, that of a teacher in the academy. He was a great believer in having a sound mind in a sound body. So was I.

Thus it went, one life after another. Each life I lived was adding its own contribution to the growing store of my skills and experiences. I passed through them all, one after another, as they flashed on the screen of my mind like the images in motion pictures. Some lives were more vivid than others, but they certainly were all interesting. All lives I had lived, I lived to the fullest, dying and passing into another body, with all of my memories and physical skills intact and active. I knew no one like myself. I may have been unique, but I did not look for others either. I was usually quite a conventional man in my society, but sometimes I was a criminal, while sometimes a minor official. The highest position I ever held was an appeals court judge. There was nothing to call much attention to myself. Public attention would not be good for me. As the saying goes, I knew too much.

The broad sweep of history passed me by in the details of ordinary peoples lives lived in various circumstances. The broad canvas of the human race was not important when one was more concerned with the price of sheep, the daily stocking of the warehouse, and the condition of the children and household. I was concerned only with my own life and myself.

Inventing my nephew who would come for me in those times I died alone was one way of passing things on from me to me. It was a most successful innovation, but I must admit it took me five hundred years to think of it. Even so, the idea of having a young nephew was not always as useful as I might have wished it to be.

Eventually, I went back to the area where the slave farm had been, or rather, to where I thought it had been. I was never sure. There was a smaller town there now, or perhaps it was larger, but smaller to my now more experienced eyes. One glance was enough. I knew there was nothing for me to be found there. I never returned.

The talents I accumulated life after life proved to be most beneficial to me. I learned to be most persuasive from an orator who worked the streets telling people stories for what coin he could collect. He was quite loquacious and very persuasive, a talent I have kept with me. Being loquacious and persuasive, I had discovered, were worthwhile talents to have.

I tried to stay in safe places, but this was not always possible. As the church went rushing through Europe in its insane way, I moved about in the middle classes, being as conventional as possible until the chance came for me to escape to Moslem Egypt. There I died and was reborn a Moslem merchant, selling flour and spice to those who cooked their family dinner. My business prospered, and my education expanded considerably. The refugees from now Christian Spain entered Egypt. I sold food and spice to them as well. I died and for the first time entered into my son, the strongest of my children, he became a merchant as well. Unfortunately, my experiment came to a bad end, as the quarreling between my sons over their inheritance came quickly to blows, and later to poison plots.

I managed to survive, but now I was far more careful of my family and my children. Sending them on impossible quests became the norm. I lived there in Egypt for some time, but eventually went west again, to enter France by crossing the sea selling cloth. From there, I went north. One life spent as a Jew convinced me living in the strict confines of a religion was not for me. I went on as a middle class Catholic in a land of middle class Catholics. Some lives were more profitable than others were, but gradually I adapted and entered only certain kinds of

IMMORTALITY

bodies. Strong and healthy, but also prosperous, either now or bound to become so in a very short time.

I came to America and began selling coal thirty years before the civil war. I ended up in New York City, which was large enough I thought it could become my permanent playground. I was fine through the war, too old to serve, and too young to sit and be idle. The idea of compulsory military service frightened me; I had no desire to ever die as a soldier. I now entered older bodies, those who could not be conscripted. They were more successful as well. Their lives were a bit shorter, but a short prosperous life was all right with me. It was possible for me to move around a bit more frequently.

Now I left no progeny, no children lived beyond me. Poison and a more modern medical education assured me of this. The nephew story was becoming more active, and more useful as well. It was obvious to all who knew me in this life I would die a loner, and so I did. I slumped in my chair and my body perished.

Death was actually occurring to my body as I leapt down to the street below, where I landed on the back of a passing man of about thirty years. I probed his mind, discarding him, but I steered him to the Wall Street area where I soon found just what I was looking for. A twenty three year old independently wealthy wimp of a stock trader, he was a man who traded on his own account. He was ideal for me. He was a perfect choice for my purposes. I was on him in a flash, riding him until he slept and I could enter into him fully. It was the evening of the day, and he thought of himself as a rake. I enjoyed watching, and as he dropped off to sleep next to a lovely woman, his companion for the evening. I entered completely into him and took over his body. This possession of the new body was easy, countless repetitions of this same action had made it quite simple for me to do this now. This was especially so with someone like him, who did not resist me at all.

My new persona had a home on the west coast. Wonderful, perhaps we could retire there shortly. I was quite ready for another life of ease. I believe I had made another good choice in selecting him to provide my new body.

Now there was no resistance left from him. The part of him he had been was cowering in a corner, frightened and fading away rapidly. His attitude suited me to a tee. I had seized his body, his physical estate, like so many others I had seized in the past. It was now my exclusive property. I was now him, and he was gone with the wind of change I had blown into him. His mind and education were mine as well. Of course, he did not know what had happened to him. It had never happened to him before. On the other hand, I was perfectly aware of what I had done to the young fool. I had accomplished this change of bodies several dozen times, if not a hundred times. I had not bothered to keep count.

I had died at seventy, and had not had a woman for some fifteen years. Naturally, once I was fully settled into this new and viral body, I reached for the slattern he had been sleeping next to. I woke her and surprised her with my passion. I was not a modern gentle lover as he had been. I was far more demanding and forceful. I rode the bitch heavily, giving her a ride she would never forget. Afterwards she curled up against me, pledging her undying love for me. I slept content.

In the morning, I took the slattern again and afterwards ordered her to make me coffee. After a cup of coffee, we had time to shower together. I sent her off to her day's activities, as she promised to return this evening. I was unconcerned with her. I had to search his apartment and become more familiar with the ideas in his mind as they translated into the physical objects in his apartment. There was no reason for me to go to the exchange today, I had plenty of money, and even more coming to me. After I had identified his things, I dressed as if I were going to the exchange. As the maid came in to clean the apartment, I left and went to the cheap SRO hotel I had lived in previously. I was now the promised well-spoken nephew of my former self.

IMMORTALITY

Fortunately, my old body had not begun to stink. The man who let me in neglected to tell me the rent was paid a month in advance, but I made funeral arrangements, a quick cremation and scattering the ashes in the sea, and I took the small assortment of worldly goods belonging to my former self. I was there and gone in an hour and a half. The valise of documents and keys to safe deposit boxes were my prime concern. My old self had now been completely disposed of.

My new self went to retrieve some of the many things I had squirreled away. I went to the exchange and 'read the tape' for a while in the members lounge. I spent just enough time there to keep me up to date. I looked in my book, I could afford to let most of my shares ride, but I would come in tomorrow and sell off the cats and dogs. I was anxious to go west and see if the house there was as lovely as the picture he had of it on his bookcase had indicated. I returned to my apartment and packed two bags. I would be ready to leave tomorrow. I noticed he had two bankers' cards in his wallet. I looked at the balances in his checkbook. Both of them were in the middle five figures. I noticed on one statement he had a middle six-figure savings account as well. He had a monthly five figure direct deposit in one of the accounts. The other was his trading account. Looking back, I saw he ran six and seven figure balances from time to time. Good there would be no problem about my putting in the funds from the stock sales. This young man had more than just plenty of money. He was quite well off indeed.

I sat in the easy chair and reviewed what he knew of himself. I well knew it was the sum of the lies he had told himself about himself, but there is always some truth behind the veil of our many self-delusions. I wanted to know all of his history, and I quickly learned it, both the true and the false.

As I was finishing up that task, the slattern knocked on the door. I let her in, sent her to the bedroom, and mated with her again in an active session convincing her she was my love slave. I told her I was going to the west coast, and if she accompanied me, it would have to be as my paid sex toy. I had heard rumors of forced common law marriages, and suits for support, later to be called palimony. I wanted nothing to do with them. I added to her, I though paying about the minimum wage for a sex toy was plenty. Naturally, she was grieved at my attitude. I added to her if she wanted to come west with me she should bring a friend, and she was doubly grieved. I smiled and told her life was hard for all of us. She left, but in a mood in which she realized she had been conquered, and the master of her body had just said he did not really need her. My attitude toward her disturbed her more than anything I could ever do to her. I was unconcerned, life is hard, and art is long. It was just six PM. There was still time for her to change her mind.

    I sat down at the desk and wrote out a contract, specifying she would be paid two hundred dollars a week, and receive room and board, in exchange for her sexual and domestic services. The wage was very generous to my mind. If she did return with a friend, it would be four hundred a week for the two of them. That was more than enough. It was quite good pay for the times. I have always considered myself a kind and generous man, but I also thought to myself, no one had ever considered me a fool.

    I had already discovered this young man had installed a fully equipped office in his home, and was a graduate of an Ivy League college and law school. His parents had put a great deal of money into his education. They had then conveniently died accidentally, leaving him on his own. Fortunately, I had made an excellent choice in selecting him. Sometimes you are lucky, other times you are not so lucky. This time I had been very lucky indeed. I was quite pleased.

    I called down to the restaurant and ordered up a decent dinner for myself. I was surprised the young man had no manservant, but I knew servants were out of style today. For this reason, and no other, I would really have preferred it if the model returned. I had already discovered he had a woman coming in during the day to clean and do laundry. She had come in today, spending an hour or two, and being surprised to find me

IMMORTALITY

at home. I had left for the SRO hotel just as she arrived, which was probably just as well. An establishment with this much money, and a house like he apparently had in California really needed to have a servant or two to take care of things.

The dinner came and I ate. I assumed the slattern was not returning, so I called the airline about flights going out to California near noon. I made a reservation, for the day after tomorrow; I would pay for it by check when I received my tickets. I realized I would have to have my mail forwarded, and take care of other things. I decided to see the concierge of the apartment building about this. This was a luxury apartment building. In terms of services, it was almost like a hotel for long-term residents.

I went to bed and to sleep. I was going to enjoy a lifetime living in the lap of luxury. The next day I sold off my cats and dogs and went to a brokerage firm where the young man had a friend working, a man whom he considered his best and closest friend. I told the man I was going to the west coast for a month or two and left the remaining portfolio in his hands. I told him I was expecting to see it increased when I returned. He said he would do what he could. We shook hands after I had filled out all of the papers, and I left. I was sure his friend would do whatever he could to make me a bit wealthier.

My next stop was at the concierge of the apartment building. He was an older gray haired man. I explained what my plans were to him. He said he would forward my mail out to me, as well as look after my apartment. I gave him a hundred dollar bill for postage, implying more would come if I were satisfied with his service. I also obtained his telephone number so I could let him know when I was returning. The slattern still had not called, so I gave up on her. It was five in the afternoon, so I decided to seek other feminine companionship.

I changed clothes, and went to a bar in the apartment building. It took me almost no time at all to locate an interested young lady. I invited her to dinner, and soon we were becoming very well acquainted indeed. She returned to my apartment with me, and we were enjoying ourselves in bed in no time at all. She had a reaction to my lovemaking very much as the slattern had. She wanted to remain with me. I made her the same offer I had made the slattern.

Instead of becoming indignant, she was amazed. She said she could not do housework, nor could she cook, but she was certainly willing to perform sexually with me. I pointed out I was going to California, and required more than just sexual satisfaction. We got out of bed and I showed her pictures of the house in California. I also showed her the contract I had made out. Adding I needed someone who was good at the cooking and housework, as well as proficient in the sexual area, I told her I was sorry she would not do.

She dressed and left, saying she wished she could cook. Oh well, apparently many New York women did not either cook or do housework. I went back to bed and slept through the night unconcerned. There were certainly enough women in California. I knew I would find one there to suit my purposes.

I had been to California once before, traveling there on the train. It had been several dozen years ago. In 1923, I believe. I had traveled to Chicago, where I had transferred to another train, going on to San Francisco. I recalled the trip, it been long and boring. Two or three nights on the train as I recall. The trip by air was much easier, although we made three stops on the way, and encountered some delays.

I rented an automobile in the airport, and drove to the house, which was now mine. It was even nicer than the pictures in his apartment had made it appear. The house had a caretaker, an older man who kept up the house, lawn, and pool. The man regularly made his coffee and breakfast in the big main kitchen. He lived on the premises in a small apartment over the large garage.

The caretakers name was Harold, and I took to him immediately. I actually liked him far more than the young man had, as he had considered the caretaker to be only a shady background figure to his own inflated ego. I decided I would

IMMORTALITY

encourage the man to talk to me. He was most willing, as I did not treat him as if he was of no importance. As far as I was concerned, he was quite important to me, keeping up this house for me was a task in itself.

From the houseman I learned the young man's father had been interested in investing in films. The young man had not followed up on this interest, but he had kept the house his father had purchased for business as a vacation retreat. The houseman believed I was here now for a vacation. It was a reasonable belief, and I was not going to challenge him with it. I mentioned I was interested in finding one or two women who would be combination housekeepers, and sex toys for myself. I added to him, if I could find some pleasing companionship, I might retire here in California permanently.

Harold told me I could easily find what I was seeking. He promised to keep his eyes open for one or two suitable women. I thanked him, telling him I knew he was far more familiar with the city than I was, and could best select someone. I noticed he warmed up to me considerably, once he saw I was interested in treating him as if he was a person of some importance to me. His attitude pleased me, as he certainly was important to me, having sole charge of this very expensive home when I was not present was a very serious responsibility indeed, at least it was in my eyes.

One thing I have noticed in the course of my many lives is the manner in which those in humble positions, even positions key to the life of their betters, are often ignored or mistreated by those who chance has placed in authority over them.

Naturally this is a great mistake on the part of those in authority, as the enmity they create in this way can easily come back to haunt or even destroy them. It always pays to be kind and considerate of those in inferior positions, as their good graces may often come to the aid of their supposed superiors in surprising ways. Having learned the lesson, from both sides of the table so to speak, I was now always polite to, and quite interested in, those who were theoretically my social inferiors. I was also sure to make it a point to be kind to everyone I encountered in the course of a lifetime. I recommend this policy to everyone, although only a few people ever seem to wish to consistently follow it.

I took my time and toured the house. It was three stories high with a full basement, and a large semi outdoor swimming pool, set on at least an acre or more of land. It was more luxurious than comfortable, and although the furnishings were slightly dated, they were more than adequate for anything I might wish to have. I knew I would be quite happy living here. The garage was suitable for three cars, one of which was the caretaker's pick up truck. There was a Ford automobile in the garage as well as another car, a German BMW. Harold assured me they were both in excellent running condition. I immediately asked about arranging to return the rented automobile. Harold said he would take care of it. I gave him the keys, and he disappeared with the car.

His absence gave me a chance to thoroughly explore the second and third floors, which were primarily full of comfortable bedrooms with attached baths. There were three large bedrooms on the third floor and two even larger ones on the second. There was an easy access to a comfortable roof deck from the third floor. The master bedroom on the second floor was actually as large as my Manhattan apartment was. The centerpiece of the master bedroom was a long and over large 'California' style bed located on a slightly elevated platform. The other bedrooms all had double beds. The more I explored this place, with which it would be assumed I was already quite familiar, the more impressed I was with it. I knew it would definitely suit me to live here for quite some time.

The young man had no good memories of this house. He seemed to think the house was a burden, and had even considered selling it. He seemed to believe the house was taking money from him he could otherwise use in speculating in the stock market. I had reviewed his record of market speculations, and while he had been reasonably successful, his returns had certainly not been outstanding. He was, like most investors, a follower of fads. Like most investors, his returns were about what bank interest would have paid him.

I was content to live here, leaving the apartment in New York available for business and infrequent social trips to the east coast. This obvious change in my plans would require an accompanying story for the houseman, and quite likely a few others. Fortunately, the young man had few real friends who would have to learn the story.

I showered and refreshed myself as I thought of the story, possibly saying I was tired of risking my fortune on the turn of the cards of the stock market. I decided I would just tell Harold I had decided I needed to sew some oats, wild or otherwise, while I was still young. He seemed to be in his late forties, or so, and I was sure he could appreciate my using this as an excuse for moving to southern California, where there was supposedly a far more liberal social scene.

The house was located just off the California coast highway, California 1, just a bit north of the limit of Los Angeles County. I would later discover it was just on the edge of the area afflicted with spells of disastrous fires and floods each year. The area was no longer fashionable, but it was safe and secure. Personally, I preferred safe and secure to fashionable any day.

The young man had provided me with a California wardrobe, from which I selected a casual shirt and some slacks. I changed clothes and was ready to see Harold return. I also discovered the young man kept several hundred dollars in his sock drawer. This common mode of thrift was interesting. I put some of the money in my wallet, and went down to the living room. The young man apparently had developed the not uncommon habit of hiding substantial sums of money in a variety of odd places.

Harold came back from the automobile rental place, and I decided I would take him out for dinner. As I did not know any of the restaurants in the area, I asked him to select where we dined. He picked a nice moderately priced restaurant for us.

Once there, he pointed out there were a number of single young ladies eating, as well as a number of them employed as waitresses. He identified these attractive women as being motion picture extras who lived in nearby rooming houses. He said he could probably get one of them to join us, and become our housekeeper. As we left the restaurant, he posted a three by five card on a notice board mentioning I was looking for a cook - housekeeper who could take care of my home. I was not optimistic about the posting, but it did seem it would be an interesting way to find someone.

We returned to the house where I watched the TV for a while before heading to bed. I had discovered the house had a full sized motion picture screening room in the basement. This was something Harold had assured me was almost standard for upscale California homes. I went off to sleep wondering where the moving pictures shown in the screening room came from. I was sure Harold would know. He seemed to be very well acquainted with such things.

The next morning, as we enjoyed breakfast, I told Harold we would have to go grocery shopping. He agreed, and together we began making a rather extensive grocery list. As we worked on the grocery list, the telephone rang and Harold answered it. I sipped my coffee and listened to him speak to someone who was calling about the position he had posted on the restaurant's notice board. Harold explained to her the duties of the position involved more than simple housekeeping, and asked if the young lady on the other end of the wire had a boy friend. Her answer apparently being suitable, he invited her to come out for an interview.

The positive response to the telephone call caused me to go to my room and obtain the legal documents I had previously written for the position. They spelled out the duties of the housekeeper in great detail, even including that she might be required to remain nude in the house, and she would be expected to be fully sexually available at all times. I read the contract over again, and decided it would be sufficiently blunt to dissuade

IMMORTALITY

anyone who was the least bit hesitant from fulfilling the various requirements I had listed on it.

We finished our grocery list, which include a small liquor list. I wanted to have the bar in the living room stocked for guests, although I only seldom drank myself. I was about to let Harold go out to pick up the groceries when the doorbell rang. The young lady who had answered the ad was at our door.

Harold let her in, and she came into the living room with a bit of trepidation. I smiled and pointed out a seat on a couch near where I was sitting, and asked her to sit. Harold said he would get us all something to drink, and fetched coffee for us. In the meantime, I had taken down the girl's name, Nancy Byrnes, her address, and social security information. She looked older than I did, not a great concern to me.

Once the three of us were settled and sipping our coffee, I began talking to her. She said she could cook, do housework, sew, and generally take care of the house. She smiled and added she had even taken a course in auto repair in high school, where she had been primarily involved in drama. Like countless other girls, she had come to Los Angeles to become an actress, but she was not either sufficiently skilled, or wealthy enough, to be able to live on the slim pickings she earned as an occasional extra in films. Her last acting stint had been last year, and had lasted only three days. In the meantime, she had been working as a prep chef in the restaurant where we had posted the notice. She was most willing to settle into a permanent position as my housekeeper.

I questioned Nancy about her age, and was surprised to find she was only twenty-three. It was the same age I was in this body. She told me she had been rather badly used in a relationship, which finished when her last job as an extra started. I supposed the stress of the relationship was what had caused her to look concerned, or care worn as I had put it to myself.

I asked her if she was aware of the other requirements of the job. She said she had an idea the use of her body would be desired as well. She said it seemed to be the normal thing here in Los Angeles, as women were hired for their sex as well as for any other skill they might have. I smiled and passed the contract to her. I waited patiently as she read it through.

Once she had, she looked at me and just said, "$200.00 a week seems a fair salary for what you are asking of me."

"I thought so." I replied. I added, "You will also receive room and board, and will live and eat with us. I am willing to have two women in this place, in this position, but no more. Now if you excuse us, I would like to talk to Harold about this and see if we can reach an agreement."

I smiled at her, and motioned to Harold. We left the room together, going into the kitchen. I asked him his thoughts. He thought she would be satisfactory, but he wanted to ask her a couple of questions. Naturally, I agreed he should question her as well. We went back to the living room and he spoke to her.

"When did you go through drug rehab, Nancy?" Harold asked her.

"When I was nineteen, I was in Rehab for a year, getting out when I was twenty. I came out here when I was eighteen and fell right into the drug scene. I got out of the drug scene when I had a bad trip and the police put me into the county rehab unit. I've been straight ever since. I don't smoke and I rarely drink. I don't use pot either. I mean I know some people don't consider it a drug, but I do now."

I wondered how Harold knew she had been involved with drugs. I had no idea. I looked at Harold and nodded, encouraging him to ask her some additional questions.

"Why don't you work as a waitress at the restaurant, I would think it would pay better." He said, smiling at her. He seemed to be happy with her answers.

"It does, but my last boyfriend got me out with something and had me tattooed. Now I'm very careful where I expose myself. Those short skirt and brief costumes at the restaurant would show my tattoo whenever the skirt was blown up. I really don't want it happening." She paused a bit. She was obviously embarrassed. "The tattoo's why I broke up with him. It was a while before I found out what he had done to me. He told me it was a big butterfly."

"What did he have tattooed on you?" I was curious, wondering how bad it could be.

"Here, I'll show you." She lifted her skirt in the rear. On the right cheek of her butt was tattooed, 'This Slut is the Property of Thomas Findlay.' The tattooing was in large bold letters, and could not be missed. She showed it to both Harold and I, then dropped her skirt looking from one of us to the other as if we might reject her because of it.

"Your tattoo is in no way a bar to your working for me." I added to reassure her. As I had thought she might, Nancy was relieved at that. Harold had no more questions, so the two of us adjourned briefly, and talked again. We decided to hire her for a two-week trial without using her sex. If she were satisfactory, we would begin using her sexually. I returned to the living room and explained this to Nancy. I added to her, regardless of her permanency, she would receive two weeks wages if she survived the first twenty-four hours with us. As additional security for her, I told her to keep her room at the boarding house for at least a month, until she was sure of her position with us. She agreed to do so.

Harold was to go to the boarding house with Nancy and help her move her things here. She said she had only a couple of suitcases and an overnight bag. They left and I went back to reading through the outdated magazines in the living room magazine rack. Some of the magazines were so old I had read them in my previous body some time ago. I wondered if there were subscriptions to these magazines. If so, I would have to cancel them. My mind turned to introspection, as it does now.

At the time this interview occurred, in the late 1940's, there were no VCR's. They were barely available in commercial television studios. An expensive tube type Black and White Television set was located in the living room. Home computers were unknown, as were many other electronic gadgets we now take for granted, cell phones, fax machines, and even telephone answering machines were far in the future. Obviously, I did not miss any of these electronic marvels that would soon become so common. Naturally, I did not miss any of these things, as I had never had access to them. I had barely even heard of the possibility of any of them.

This experience occurred in another time, a time of different causes and different interests. I was unconcerned with any of these public concerns. My sole desire was for stability, luxury, and sensuality. I had not enjoyed a great deal of that sort of thing lately, and I was quite ready to indulge myself in it.

I recall that I thought Nancy's body was not exceptional. She was a worker, not a glamour girl, or a sex queen. What I needed first was a worker. The sex queen would likely be another acquisition. She could come along later, once the worker was well established. Thinking of Nancy as a worker made me think of the harvest song, 'Work for the night is coming.' It had been a very long time since I had heard it. I smiled at the memory.

I heard the truck pull into the drive, or I thought I did. It was some time before I heard Harold and Nancy come into the house. Either he had been talking to her or he had used her sexually. I was unconcerned with either. A woman's sexual facilities do not wear out. Her body may age, but like a man, her mind, and mental reactions will usually remain what once they were, at least until she is quite aged. Disease is all we ever fear, which reminded me I would have to have her tested by a physician for venereal infections.

After Harold showed Nancy to the second floor room where she would stay, he came down and asked me if I was interested in pursuing another woman at this time. I told him I thought it best if we allowed Nancy to settle in first, unless he had someone in mind. He did. He had a long time girlfriend he would be interested in moving into his quarters. He had spoken to her, and she was quite willing to move in with him. He added almost apologetically, she and Nancy had seemed to get on well. I told him to bring her in and I would talk to her. She came in

IMMORTALITY

nude. She was completely unembarrassed, and quite comfortable with her nudity. She was also at least thirty-five or forty, possibly older, being much closer to Harold's age than to the age of either Nancy or my present body.

Her name was Lucy Arnold, and she had been going out with Harold for some time. They had discussed moving in together, but Harold had been unsure of the reaction of his employer, who had previously seemed to be a bit touchy, so he had never mentioned it to him. I told the two of them it would be all right with me, but if she worked for us, she should be sexually exclusive with Harold, while Nancy would be sexually exclusive with me. This arrangement was also satisfactory. I drew up a contract specifying her working with Harold, under his direction, doing housework and outside work, such as gardening, and be paid $200.00 per week, as well as receiving her room and board.

The arrangement was most agreeable to both of them. While I was at it, I raised Harold's salary to $250.00 per week from the $125.00 he had been making. A better salary, actually an excellent salary for the times, would keep them both well paid and content. A pay roll of $650 per week was about the maximum I wished to have however.

Nancy came downstairs nude. Like many women, she looked better nude than clothed. She announced she was all moved in. Harold had picked up his girl friend Lucy when he had brought Nancy's things, but being uncertain of my reaction, he had not moved her in. I suggested he go grocery shopping with her, and get her things to move her in as well. She was also a motion picture extra, and she lived at the same rooming house Nancy did. I thought that was convenient, but I said nothing about it to them. I did wonder when she had worked last. After I gave him two hundred dollars for groceries, Harold and Lucy went to his truck, Lucy dressed, and they left. I asked Nancy to throw out all of the old magazines and other trash lying around the house. Then I sat in the living room, intending to watch television for a while. It was afternoon, and there was only a weak soap opera on. The lack of interesting television programs convinced me to go swimming.

The pool was enclosed by the house on three sides, and had a roof, and a glass and aluminum accordion wall, which could be used to close off the fourth side. The accordion wall was open today, as it was quite nice out. I went to the pool and leaving my clothes on a nearby chair, entered it slowly. The water was warm, but not hot. I swam for a while, and noticed Nancy come into the poolroom. I told her she could swim with me if she wished. She disappeared, shortly returning with an armload of towels. Once the towels were on the table at the side of the pool she dove in neatly. She was an excellent swimmer. I swam better than my body had swum in this life. It was a few minutes until my better swimming skills were being reflected in this body.

Once I was comfortable swimming, I began swimming laps. I was surprised to find the musculature of my body appeared not to have been used recently. I realized the former occupant had devoted himself exclusively to trading on the exchange floor, to the point where he had neglected the remainder of his life. It was no time at all until I was exercising my body as I was used to doing. I have always liked having a strong and well-exercised body, and I intended to gain one and maintain it. I decided then I would make a point of exercising every day.

Nancy swam laps alongside me for some time. She was quite happy swimming. Obviously she was as athletically inclined as I was. She got out first, but I swam four or five more laps before I left the pool. We sat together at the pool table, wiping our faces with one of the towels she had provided.

"Would you like me to get you something to drink?"

"Not yet, let's just sit here briefly until we catch our breath."

"That was fun, I haven't been swimming for years."

"Well, living here you can swim every day." I smiled at her.

IMMORTALITY

"That would be very nice, I truly miss swimming and exercising."

"Harold said there was a small gymnasium or exercise room somewhere in the basement. I really haven't explored the entire basement. I know it goes under the garage as well as under the house."

"This is a big place."

"Five large bedrooms, the living room and dining room, kitchen, pool, pantry, laundry room and the storage shed for the lawn care things. There's an apartment over the three-car garage where Harold lives. I think the lot's an acre or so." It was also an odd design, but I did not say it, I just casually wondered why it had been built in this rather strange way. However, I didn't learn the answer.

"It's nice. I'm sure I'll like living here."

"I hope so, I don't like the idea of changing staff, I like to have people stay with me forever." I heard her slight chuckle at my words. As I looked at her, I thought of something. "Would you do me a favor?"

"If I can, what would you like?"

"Don't cut your hair. You have nice hair, and I'd like to see how long it will grow out."

"Very well, I used to let it grow long, but when I worked in the kitchen, it was hard to keep out of things, so I cut it. Sure, I'll be happy to let it grow. I'll keep it long now." She smiled as she spoke, and it was as if sunshine broke through clouds. She was really quite attractive. I smiled back at her.

"Thank you, I think you'd look even nicer if you had long hair."

We relaxed in the pool chairs for a while and later went back to the living room. I dressed first, and followed her in. Nancy brought me coffee just as Harold and Lucy returned. She went into the garage to assist them in putting the groceries into the house. I looked around the room. There were no magazines to be seen. I wondered if Harold had brought a newspaper. I asked him. He told me he hadn't thought of it. I told him that was just as well, then tuned on the TV, and watched the news program until dinner was ready.

As I had asked, all four of us ate together. Nancy had roasted a chicken. It was really quite good. Any doubts I had about her being able to cook were quickly disappearing. She could roast a chicken, which was a very good start at cooking as far as I was concerned.

I believe it is difficult for those who have not missed many meals to understand how much l loved to eat. Over the course of my many lifetimes, I have missed very many meals. I have been so hungry I have actually become sick when I tried to resume eating. For me, eating was more than just gaining nourishment, there was a real joy present within me when I was being fed. In my mind, eating was almost a religious experience. I actually prayed in joy as I was eating, each time I ate a meal I silently thanked God I was eating once again.

I know this must sound strange to a well-fed American, but to me, it was the only way to eat. I could still remember eating small bits of meat only once a year when I was a porter. I recalled eating what odd scraps of food I could salvage in the plague ravaged France of the Middle Ages. Food was precious to me, and I rejoiced I was able to eat a meal. I did not like to ever waste food, although I had grown accustomed to the social usage that made wasting food almost a necessity from time to time.

I was glad when the pre World War One custom of leaving food on the plate was banished forever. It had always disturbed me to be so wasteful of food for those few decades when it was an accepted social usage. Now I always tried to clean my plate. As I did, I often recalled those many times when I had not had a plate to clean, much less anything to eat.

I interject this, because my opinion was strongly pitched against those who wasted food. I was happy to note than none of the other three at the table wasted their food. Nancy particularly, seemed to be quite careful about eating everything, and neatly packing away any food that happened to be left over. I

IMMORTALITY

believe watching her put food away was when I decided she would do for me. As I said, the way people deal with food has always been quite important to me.

The first two days passed quickly, and although Nancy purchased a cookbook, she was already a good cook as far as I was concerned. Breakfast lunch and dinner were made and served without incident. Harold and Lucy took care of the bulk of the house and grounds, while all four of us went swimming several times a day. It was really quite a pleasant life.

As such a pleasant life does, it quickly became boring. I began taking trips around town, just looking at the sights. Air pollution being what it was in the late 1940's, I only took these trips on days when there was little or no pollution, rare as those days were in the Los Angeles area. I took Nancy with me on most of my trips, visiting the La Brea tar pits, the various museums, and other such sights of the city. We also toured the motion picture studios, not my primary interest, but which I found interesting nonetheless. I also traveled up the coast highway, and visited many of the sights on the highway between Los Angeles and San Francisco. Nancy and I also visited San Francisco occasionally, once spending an entire week there, just enjoying ourselves.

Naturally, by this time, Nancy and I had become lovers. I found her to be a most satisfactory lover, and as I was quite content with her, I decided not to expand my search for another carnal entertainer. I found her to be both a pleasant companion, and an interesting and responsive mate.

With Harold's assistance, I had located where motion pictures that could be shown in the private screening room came from. I rented several to show in the screening room in the basement. We soon gave up the idea however, as none of us were sufficiently interested in the movies to continue to watch them. Harold had a small collection of movie posters, the extent of his interest in the industry. I learned he had once drawn these posters, in one of the studio art shops. Most of the posters he had collected were those either he or a friend of his had drawn.

VARMUS

While now considering myself a California native, I did return to New York two or three times for short visits. On one of these trips east, Nancy accompanied me. We spent a couple of weeks, enjoying the sights of the city as much as any other tourist couple ever had. It was during that trip I decided to sell my exchange membership, and close out all of my holdings in New York. I easily accomplished this task. The last thing to go was the apartment. I actually had very little to move to California, most of the things in the apartment were best used as charitable donations, and tax deductions. I got rid of these things, and soon I was living in California full time.

In most stories of this kind, there is always some kind of tragedy or upset, which occurs, giving the plot of the story a sudden twist of some kind. In my tale, this does not occur. My life went on the same smooth path until mid 1972, when Harold retired. He was sixty-five and eligible for the social security pension.

Naturally, I encouraged both he and Lucy to stay with me, but they wished to return to Arkansas where Harold apparently either had a home or had maintained family roots of some kind. They had saved most of their salary, so they were both well provided for. Nancy and I saw them off, and the following day I hired a lawn service to take care of the pool and grounds. It was a great deal less expensive than what I had been paying Harold and Lucy. Nancy cleaned up his apartment and sealed it off, awaiting the next tenant, which I had no idea of ever engaging.

Nancy and I lived together for several more years, and although we are growing old together, we are both quite content with our lives. I have already picked out the young neighbor boy as someone I wish to enter into when I die. He is another attractive athletic lad, at present only fifteen years of age. I have discussed making him my heir with his parents, and they are thrilled with the idea. I have arranged my will so the boy will be the legitimate inheritor of my entire estate. So all is prepared for my easy departure from this life in a few years, say when he is

IMMORTALITY

twenty-one or two. Naturally, Nancy will die first, my carefully made poisons will assist me to insure I survive her. I have discovered I much prefer being well off to being poor. I have decide to continue living a few more lives in this far more comfortable vein. I think in a few more years, probably another decade, I shall be ready to go. I am enjoying my life now, and there is certainly no need for me to rush things.

The Tale of the Coachman of Paris

This story was told me in a men's club, where I had been invited to have dinner with a number of casual acquaintances. The conversation had deliberately been turned to alchemy by the host; an inquiry was made of me as to whether I knew any alchemists. Naturally, I denied I knew any, as I knew quite well the motive underlying the question. In fact, I knew three alchemists, none of whom would be at all interested in meeting the kind of adventurers and schemers my curious dinner companions actually happened to be, regardless of what they thought of themselves.

My denial of knowledge of any alchemists, being accepted, the host, Frank Reardon, began telling the following tale, which he swore was true. He said it had even been published in an academic journal, although he could not recall the name of the journal, or when it had been published. I found the tale interesting, and as it fully agreed with what I little I had heard of the so-called draught of immortality, or elixir of life. I shall tell the tale here so it may not be lost, being previously published in some unknown academic journal or not.

In Paris, a decade or so before the revolution, there was a marquise and his wife who both had carnal interests apart from

IMMORTALITY

their legitimate interests at home. The wife of the marquise was accustomed to be driven to the bower of her lover twice each week in a coach. One of the coachmen would wait in the shop of a nearby pharmacist, with whom he had developed a friendship. They would talk, smoke a pipe, and have a sip of beverage while the woman and her lover performed their romantic athletics in the lovers abode.

Now the pharmacist was very interested in alchemy, something of which he made no secret. As a maker of medicines, he was more interested in finding the universal medicine, the alchemical elixir of life, than he was in changing base metals to gold. As he had explained to the coachman numerous times, this medicine would make all other medicines obsolete, as it would immediately and instantly cure any disease, and heal any physical complaint, as well as be a tonic beyond compare for the person who was fortunate enough to have access to it.

Naturally, the coachman who was in his forties and suffered from some arthritic complaints as well as the usual coughs and colds, was quite interested in this marvelous medicine. Hearing of it, he asked the pharmacist to give him enough to help cure him of his aching bones, so he could better perform his tasks. The pharmacist, anxious to test out his medicine, assured his friend he would be one of the very first to gain the advantage of its rare benefits, as soon as he had finally made this marvelous medicine.

As the wife played with her lover, the friendship between the pharmacist and the coachmen gradually deepened. In time, as the year passed, the pharmacist told the coachman he felt he was getting closer to the discovery of the universal medicine he so avidly sought. Naturally, the coachman congratulated him, and urged him forward on this path of discovery of the very elixir of life.

One day, when the coachman entered the pharmacist's shop, he was greeted with the wild shout of the pharmacist telling him he had made the universal medicine at last. The pharmacist came out from his back room carrying a wine glass almost full of reddish tinged liquor, apparently a cordial of some kind. He assured his friend this was the so-called universal medicine, the very elixir of life itself. The coachman was struck dumb by the enthusiasm of his friend, and by the very ordinary appearance of the supposedly miraculous elixir, residing in the plain wine glass the pharmacist held in his hand.

"Here now Marcel, for your arthritis and joint pains, take a sip now. Only a small sip you will need to cure you of your difficulty forever."

The pharmacist held the wine glass out to his friend, who took it and sipped a tiny bit from the glass, before handing it back to his friend.

"It tastes like a cordial of some odd flavor I cannot identify."

"It is the very elixir of life itself, Marcel, it will allow me to live forever." So saying, the pharmacist took the entire remaining contents of the wine glass into his mouth, and swallowed it down. The liquid hardly had time to reach his stomach before the inventive druggist was struck down as if by an invisible bolt. As his lifeless body crashed to the floor, the glass he had held shattered, spilling the last few drops of the solution, which had slain the unfortunate man.

At the same instant, the poor coachman felt his bowels release. He soiled himself; such as he had not done since he was a child. He staggered out the door of the pharmacist's shop and called to his companion, who was watering the horses, still attached to the coach. Attracting the attention of his companion, the coachman fell insensible to the ground.

The lady who was their passenger came from her assignation to find her coachman was unconscious, and had soiled himself several times. He had been placed on the coachman's rack, where his associate held on to him as he drove the coach back to the home of the marquise. There the other coachman was able to obtain some assistance, and the unconscious man was brought to his room and attended to with some difficulty. He was cleaned of his foulness, and put to bed, where his condition was noted as being unconscious and with slight and shallow respiration. The wife of the marquise inquired of the coachman and the other staff, initially thinking he had taken too much drink. She was assured it was not drink; the coachman had developed a sudden illness of some kind.

The man was treated as well as possible, and his recovery was anticipated, although it did not happen for quite some time. In fact, all of his hair fell out and all of his teeth left his mouth. This event caused a physician to be called to see to him, in the fear there possibly was some kind of disease present. The physician recommended honey water and broth to be given to the man whenever he woke. This meant one of the servants who were off duty was required to watch over the coachman to feed him and care for him as well as possible, monitoring him both day and night.

There followed a period of some months, while the coachman slowly recovered from his severe debility. Naturally, in this time, the wife of the marquise possibly learned of the death of the pharmacist, or possibly, she did not. Whether or not she was concerned with it, or connected this death with the illness of her coachmen is unknown, although I believe it highly unlikely. There is certainly no recorded comment of her having any interest at all in the health of either the pharmacist or of her coachman.

It was decided at the death tax hearing the pharmacist had poisoned himself through the misapplication of some unknown medicine he was making. The presence of the coachman in the pharmacists shop at the time was unknown, and thus unremarked on. The other coachman did not mention it, as he thought the illness his companion suffered was due to either bad food or bad liquor he had received from the hand of the pharmacist. As a loyal co-worker, he did his best to hide any minor misadventure on the part of his companion from their employer.

Two or three months after he first took to bed, the coachman was able to get up and briefly walk around his room before returning to his bed to sleep once again. His new teeth were coming in, causing him great pain. His hair was growing out again, so he did not look to be bald any longer. He was still on a diet of broth and honey water, and he stayed on the meager diet for the next three months or more. In the fourth or fifth month after he was first bedridden, he began to eat solid foods again. His mouth and teeth were sore, and his hair was soon over long, but it did seem to him his arthritic joints were now less painful, if not completely pain free.

He needed exercise, and in the fourth or fifth month from his initial decumbenture, he began working in the coach house again, starting with washing the coaches and doing whatever other work, he could manage. After seven or eight months, he was completely back into the swing of things once again, being very grateful to the marquise and his wife for the care they had given him during the long period of his illness.

Frank Reardon continued this tale, more seriously now, were that possible.

"We now come to the period of eighteenth century French history when all becomes muddled in the stress of the approaching revolution. It was not yet that the guillotine began the reign of terror, and the blood of the nobility was spilled in the streets of Paris. However, there was unrest, there was talk of revolution, and all those of the nobility who had any foresight at all were quickly leaving France for more pleasant and far safer climes. It seemed the marquise had noble relatives who lived in Austria. He decided he would take his family there. He loaded up two carriages and started on the journey. For whatever reason, it seems he left behind the coachman who is the subject of our interest. The coachman remained along with several of the other servants who would not be going to Austria with this noble family. The Marquise left, taking his wife and his valuables with him."

"The nobleman leaves our story at this point, as there is no report of him reaching Austria, nor is their any contrary record saying he did not. He left for Austria at a providential time, taking with him, what he though was important, and this is all we can say about him."

"The coachman of our story stayed in Paris, and along with the other servants, operated the house to the best of their ability even when the new national assembly confiscated it. The new owners made the house into a residence for those who had friends in the government. The coachman stayed on, as new coaches were coming in and out of the establishment all the time. He wore new uniforms, or plain clothing, depending on the republican or more exotic sentiments of the current master of the house, or of the passenger who was riding in the coach."

"Thus in 1814, we find him still attached to the house as a coachman, and still performing the same function which he first performed there as a youth in 1727. It was at this point the master of the servants, or the butler, depending on the title you assign the senior servant of the household, noticed the coachman had neither aged nor died, as he had quite reasonably had been expected to do by this time. He questioned the man, but received no satisfactory reply from him as to the cause of this oddity."

"Now you must understand this coachman, who is the focus of our tale, while illiterate, was also likely operating at the very peak of his intellectual ability. He was in a word, somewhat dull of mind as well as being both illiterate and generally uneducated. This is not at all a criticism or condemnation of him; it is intended as a simple statement of fact. The man was holding the highest possible position he could hold in the world, and he was doing quite well with the position he held."

"The senior servant, if we may thus refer to him, told the story of this apparently ageless coachman in a tavern near the house, and as tales will, this tale was carried everywhere, usually as a pieces of choice fiction, by the usual cadre of tavern idlers and gossips. You must also understand there are those in this world whose business it is to keep their ear to the ground concerning such strange stories. Of people such as these, it is best to say nothing at all, except to point out, that in truth, they do exist. As would be expected, the story of the ageless coachman of Paris soon came to the attention of one of these curious men. He investigated the tale and found it to be, to the limit of his knowledge, true."

"The man who first heard this tale, or one of his associates, soon traced the story to the ground. Thus, it came about one day in 1815 or 16; a man presented himself with a companion at the door of the proper house. After some verbal interchange, the two men took the old coachman away with them. The old man, who still looked to be about forty, was never seen again."

"Now this is but one facet of the story, as Louis Brevalult, the reasonably well-known architect who achieved some fame under Napoleon the Third, was a student in the school of the French Academy then. You may have seen his sketches for the facade of the Montmarte Tabernacle building, as they were recently published in a new edition. In any event, he was going about Paris making sketches of various common folk. This occurred, say, in or around 1812 through 1814. I have here a photograph of one of these sketches, taken from his sketchbook, which is held in the Académie des Arts. Moreover, this other is a photograph of the reverse side of the same sketch."

As the two photographs made their way around the table, I was sure where this argument was heading. Frank Reardon, or someone close to him, had established something they considered visual proof of the long life of this coachman. I looked at the photograph, and noted the inscription on the reverse, stating it was the coachman of the house of the speaker of the assembly. I passed on the photographs, awaiting Mr. Reardon's continuation of the tale. It did not take long, as I was one of the last to view the two photographs."

"Should you not recall," Mr. Reardon continued, "in 1946, there was a gala opening of the French national opera, partly in celebration of the end of the war, which had occurred a

IMMORTALITY

year earlier, and partly in celebration of the restoration of the national opera of France. Every horse drawn carriage in Paris was pressed to service at the event, and coachmen were even imported from the provinces to handle all demands for those who could drive a coach and four. I call your attention to this photograph, enlarged as it has been, of the third carriage in the procession, carrying the finance minister of the republic and some of the leading financiers of the time. Please forgive me, this photograph shows only the faces of the two coachmen, as it is the coachman whom we are discussing is it not?"

As I had expected, the photograph showed the face of the same man as was to be seen in the sketch. I wondered if a more recent proof was to be offered, and silently hoped it would not be. I could think of no good rebuttal to this argument, except to say that many people look quite a bit alike making it easy to mistake one for the other. I was certain Mr. Reardon could not accept my argument as a worthy rebuttal. He was too interested in proving to us the long life of this humble coachman. I was also quite sure he was interested in obtaining some of this elixir of life for himself. I expected to hear quite soon of a generous offer being made by him for some of the fluid."

"Now I have one more proof for you gentlemen. This photograph was taken in Nancy, on the festival of Fat Tuesday, but two years ago. Again, this photograph has been enlarged, and arranged to show only the faces of the coachmen. Please note so far as physical appearances are concerned, it certainly seems to be the same man."

As the photograph came to me, I saw indeed, it was the same man, or at least, it certainly appeared to be him. I passed the photograph back to the head of the table. I was expecting Mr. Reardon to make his offer now. I was certain I would not be disappointed.

THE COACHMAN OF PARIS

"Gentlemen, you are all men who are aware of the various undercurrents of society. I have had an investigator seeking this man for two years. The man has vanished without a trace, and further he is unknown among those who rent or lease coaches in both Paris and Nancy. Yet, there is positive evidence from these photographs he is still alive. I will pay a substantial reward to anyone who can provide me any information concerning this man. I would like to speak to him, regardless of his apparent native stupidity."

"In addition, should any of you hear about the existence of a true alchemist, or the possibility of anyone manufacturing this so called elixir of life, I would be pleased to pay a substantial sum for any information any of you can provide me leading to them. If I am able to actually successfully find and take this elixir of life, on my recovery, I will be quite happy to pay another very substantial cash bonus for every scrap of information which has led me to attain such a happy occasion."

Mr. Reardon smiled and looked around the table at us all. I thought to myself it was highly unlikely he would ever attain his goal but he might well be fed scraps and bits of information for several years as a lure. I certainly could give him nothing at all, as I knew nothing. The alchemists I knew worked with the medicinal alchemy of herbs, and while they made alchemical medicines, I doubted they were interested in making any of this elixir of life, especially for sale to someone other than another alchemist.

Naturally, we all paid for our meal by promising to forward any information concerning either alchemy or the elixir of life to Mr. Reardon as soon as we might come across any. With our dinner party concluded, our group soon broke up. I left the men's club, making my way home on the subway.

I decided I should not call the alchemists of my acquaintance, to warn them of this effort to search them out. Instead, fearing a tap on my telephone line, I went to visit one at his apartment in midtown a day or so later. After the usual pleasantries, I mentioned to him my concern about his security, saying it

IMMORTALITY

was at risk through the curiosity of Mr. Reardon. He nodded and showed me a paper he happened to have concerning the complexities of the dosage of the elixir of life. He added only a small drop of the elixir was useful for most people, as a small amount protected them against most illnesses, but it did not either extend their life greatly or cause the debilitating condition requiring their being closely attended to for some months. He looked at me and mentioned serious illness, even a painful illness, was often a gift from the creator, and avoiding natural death through the use of life enhancing medications was actually often a curse to the person who did so. I must admit I fully agreed with him in his belief.

As I went home on the subway in the afternoon, I was reminded of the story of Alexander the Great and his search for the fountain of eternal life. On finding it, he was warned by a deathless crow of the true perils those who lived long lives might actually encounter. After thousands of years of life, the immortal crow wished only to die, but with molted wings, a broken beak, and a sightless eye, the ancient crow had discovered it could not.

As a result of this meeting, I began in my own way, to return to my earlier sorting out of the tales of those who lived to great age, and those who had taken the draught of supposedly eternal life. Most of the information I have collected in this odd endeavor is given in this book, for whatever interest or use it may be to anyone. I have also added the information above I received from my alchemist friend, which does not explain either the potent or dose, but does delve into the complexity of dosing this remarkable, and to me still entirely theoretical, universal medicine, the alchemical elixir of life.

6

A Tale of the Elixir of Life

The following story was told me by a charming gentleman who I met in New York City thirty or so years ago. Of indeterminate age, he appeared to me to be about forty years of age at the oldest. He was a well-built man, stocky, and muscular appearing. He looked as if he were a successful merchant or possibly a builder. I noted he had a full head of dark hair, and brown eyes. His appearance was neither particularly handsome nor stylish, but rather that of a solid and well established person who has seen much of life for his years.

I met this interesting man in a café, where fortune had it, because of the crowding we shared a table. I immediately noticed his eyes had the look of someone who was much older than his apparent age. I asked him gently if he had been involved in the horrors of the Second World War. From his apparent age, I thought to myself he would have had to be a child at the time, something that does not separate one from the horrors of war.

He smiled and asked me why I questioned him. I told him, relating my words to the condition of his eyes, where the abundance of lines surrounding them told me they had seen much of the ugly side of human life, things most people do not even dream of ever seeing.

IMMORTALITY

He rewarded my comment with a smile and commented favorably on my perceptiveness. We entered into a friendly conversation, such as any two strangers might do when first meeting. He told me he had come to New York from his home in Moderna Italy, to attempt to sell a book he had written to an American publisher. He explained that two publishers had already rebuffed him, although he added he still had a half dozen more publishers to see. He said he was well aware no publisher in Italy would touch his book, as he said it violated church doctrine in several unacceptable ways.

Having tried unsuccessfully for some time to find a publisher to whom I could sell a book of my own, I knew what difficulties he faced. I mentioned my own search for a publisher to him, and soon we were almost compatriots in the frustrating world of the new author seeking a publisher. Naturally, this led to our inquiring of each other what the subjects of our books were. I explained mine concerned the process of keeping one's non-physical body free of negative influences. I told him I had titled it 'Spiritual Cleansing.' My new friend mentioned his book was the tale of a man born in the eighth century, who has his life extended, without his permission, for what he eventually believes may well be an almost infinite time. He had not selected a title for his book as yet, but was calling it, 'A History Lesson.'

I smiled, and meaning to be humorous, said, "Ah, you wish to sell your autobiography."

"As a matter of fact, it is," He smiled at me. "Have you made a lucky guess? Or do you have some reason for believing it to be so?"

"Mostly it was a lucky guess, although I still believe your eyes reveal to me you're someone who has seen a great deal more of life than your physical appearance seems to indicate."

"You are very perceptive. However, I must ask you how you can so easily accept the idea a man could be a thousand years old, or possibly more, and still be seated with you here in this restaurant having a quiet cup of coffee? I doubt that many people could accept such information as easily as you seem to."

A TALE OF THE ELIXIR OF LIFE

"Perhaps it is because I have certain unusual but quite natural visual abilities, not usually developed in most people. It may also be because I am used to dealing with unusual people, including some of those very rare beings, which are actually quite far from the normal run of human life. I have seen much, although certainly not as much as you have, but my interest has always been focused on certain odd corners of humanity."

"Very well, would you like to read my autobiography?"

"To be very honest, I would be more interested in learning of the process you went through to become a so called immortal." I explained to him I was not interested in the material used, I was interested in the process, as I understood it was one of great pain and involved the almost complete vulnerability of the subject for several months.

"Well, this is the easiest thing in the world to tell you about. I will simply take a few pages from my manuscript, and we shall have them copied across the street. You shall then have the full story of the difficult passage from mortal to so-called immortal. Indeed, you are right the process is one of great pain, and complete vulnerability. Today it is far easier than it was in my time, as there are modern solutions used to feed the person intravenously while they pass through the worst of these changes. In addition, it is now possible to give them sedatives, so they remain unconscious, and do not feel the extreme pains of the process. The time taken is quite accurate, as I am told from three to six months is usually required to complete the transformation. During this time the person going through the change is completely open and vulnerable to any misadventure that may come to them."

"I have a friend who is an alchemist, while he is uninterested in the elixir of life, he has told me the dosage prescribed is of the utmost importance."

"Your friend is correct. The older the person the lesser the dose, there is an age limit, as those who are passed forty are almost never given the potent. It is best if those who are to be given the potent are dosed when they are in their early or mid

IMMORTALITY

twenties. A very complex formula is used to calculate the proper dosage, depending on the precise purity of the potent. By the way, I do not know this formula, or the composition of the potent used." He paused, looking at me intently as of he waited for my question. I demurred asking one, and he went on.

"You must understand I am only partly aware of the complexities of this process, as the dosing and treating of people to be made immortal is not at all what I do with my time. In fact, I spend most of my time, in blocks of twenty to forty years, as a small businessman. There I am busy grubbing for money, just as everyone else in the world. The making and dosing of people, either for health or so called immortality, is quite far from anything with which I am concerned. It certainly has nothing at all to do with my business. Of course, I have heard of the process occasionally, usually from some of the people I have associated with over the years."

"You are indicating the creating of immortals is still going on." I said with some amazement. I had not expected to hear this. While I had thought it a myth, I was prepared to believe it might have happened in some ancient time. However, I was surprised to find it was still occurring today.

"Why yes, but for the most part, these people who are only what we might call age extended. The object in most cases is to extend the person's age at death to four or five hundred years. Should the person seem to be satisfactory after a couple of centuries, it is possible their life will be further extended, if this is what is desired. Of course, none of this is really any of my affair either. However, I do manage to interact with some of these more knowledgeable people from time to time. As a result, I am aware of many of these things although they are not at all close to my own field of my affairs."

"Well, from what you tell me, I am far over the age at which my life might be extended anyway, so I have no need to speculate on this."

"How old are you, if I may ask."

"As I sit here with you today, I am sixty six years old."

A TALE OF THE ELIXIR OF LIFE

"Well, as I have heard the tale from those who know such things, even the slightest drop of the pure potent would likely cause your immediate death. Once someone is past forty years of age, extending his or her life is only very rarely done. Even when it is attempted, it is a very chancy affair, and it is always far more dangerous than it is for someone who is extended when they are in their twenties or the first few years of their thirties."

He moved himself in his chair as if thinking, and took a sip of coffee. "You see the potent is neither overly difficult, much less is it impossible to make. However, because of the dosage, which must be very carefully adjusted, the usual result of the person taking the potent is their very rapid death. When the potent is used as a healing remedy, something remarked on in a variety of published spiritual tracts and occult books, as well as numerous times in other more mundane literature, the amount given is very small. In these cases, the potent is usually diluted with water, alcohol, or sometimes with a mixture of both. When quantities of less than the small drop forming on the end of a fine wire are being given, dilution is always necessary. However, this healing dosage is too small to have any really upsetting effects on the person." He smiled at me, as I finished my coffee.

"There are people who have made this science their very long life's study, but I assure you I am not one of them. My interest in these things is only the interest of someone who has been a curious, but only a casual and accidental penetrator into this very complex field."

"You are indicating to me there is a group of these long lived people, are you not?"

"Why yes, but I will also tell you, when I found them they were far less concealed than they are today, and even so, it took me thirty five years of full time dedicated searching for clues of them before I managed to find the slight trace which eventually led me to them. Of course, once I met with them, after a few years of testing and trial they accepted me into their number as a friend and associate, but not exactly as a confident.

IMMORTALITY

I am in sporadic contact with them, but I am hardly a member of their councils, much less do I have a vote in their affairs. On the other hand, I am occasionally of use to them in more prosaic ways. I may serve as a messenger, or undertake some task for them. I am always happy to do these things for them. They have helped me in the past, just as I help them. I have no idea how old these people are, or the nature of their interest in worldly affairs. Incidentally, I don't advise you search for them. It would be a waste of your time."

"I do not intend to search for them, although I have heard of a wealthy man who apparently went off with the aim of discovering such people in mind." I was thinking of the late Miles Conrad, who had made no secret he was looking for those who he said, 'lived forever and controlled the world.' He had ended up in Geneva Switzerland, and had taken a flight from there to a city in Italy, when he had a fatal heart attack in mid air. This mans words put a different slant on the affair, although as I can recall the Italian police had investigated the case quite thoroughly. Several clients of mine had encouraged his search, even contributing to it financially. They all believed his death was a very normal one, brought on by the stress of his search. Now I began to wonder about this.

"I can tell you he will find no trace of them, although they will drain his funds while he searches for them." The man grinned at me. "These people all have a sense of humor you see. They lay false clues and prepare time wasting snares for the unwary. They will also be prepared to take good money for giving out bad information."

We had both finished our coffee, so we crossed the street to the quick print and copy shop on the corner. My new friend found the proper pages and pulled three or four pages from his manuscript. We had them Photostatted. He gave the copies to me. I thanked him for them and folded them away in my pocket. He also gave me a verbal explanation of where this tale begins, which I reproduce below. We exchanged addresses, and parted.

~-~

A TALE OF THE ELIXIR OF LIFE

We later exchanged Christmas cards several times, but with the increasing postage rates, I stopped sending Christmas cards overseas, as I could no longer afford to do so. Thus, I had completely lost track of this interesting man by the time Frank Reardon made his rather blunt offer in desire of having his own life extended. Frank was at least fifty and probably closer to sixty when he offered a reward for information concerning the process of life extension I mentioned earlier. He was probably to old to take advantage of anything he would find anyway.

This text is all that remains of the interesting man I met over thirty years ago. As far as I know, he was never able to have his book published. I consider this to be a shame, as it probably would have been as interesting as those later books dealing with vampires, witches, reincarnated mummies, and other supposed immortals that have been written by Mrs. Ann Rice, or those delightfully inaccurate but vastly entertaining stories written of the fictional young magician in training, Mr. Harry Potter.

The Mans Interesting Tale Begins Here

"This story begins when I was employed as a servant in a remote house in northwestern Italy, having, under some unusual circumstances arrived there after fleeing life in a monastery. My companion servant had just died, apparently, I now believe, from an overdose of the liquid supposed to prolong his life, although I have no real knowledge of the true circumstances of his death. The older man who was the owner or master of the house had arranged for a rather young woman to come into the house to become the cook. He also used her sexually, and was adamant about warning me not to touch her in a sexual way. At the time, I was, in fact, uninterested in woman. Now I would find my lack of interest, forcibly taught me in the monastery I had entered before puberty, to be quite odd in a youth. Teaching me to fear and avoid women at all costs had made up a good part of my monastic training.

IMMORTALITY

Aside from mass, in the monastery I saw no one but my teacher and fellow pupils. I was not allowed to speak during mass, so I did not. Several swift slaps and blows had insured my silence everywhere except in the classes, where I was only allowed to speak in answer to questions. My eyes were still disciplined by the monastery, I never looked directly at anyone, nor did I ever look about myself with random curiosity. Either my eyes were on the ground, or on the work, I was doing.

Of course, when I was a young boy living on a farm, the animals had sex, and I had seen them copulating. However, at the monastery I was sent to when I was about five or six, I was taught the coupling between men and women was the vilest thing there was, and I should avoid even thinking of women as anything but the source of my potential eternal damnation. The brothers had taught my even touching a woman was to immediately condemn myself to the eternal fires of hell. Because of this indoctrination, I was quite literally afraid of women.

The service of my hands was all was ever either wanted, or asked for, both in the house I was now employed, and at the monastery, I had left. Naturally, I did whatever work I could for my present master. As a household servant, I cleaned the building and courtyard as thoroughly as I could each day.

This continued until shortly after midwinter the year of 765, when the master called me and asked me to sample a drug he had made. I was to take the small flask to my room, and there drink it down after I had used the chamber pot. Once I had that simple task accomplished, I was to get myself into my bed and rest. I did as I was directed, and lay in my bed for a few moments wondering what this was all about, before I drifted off to a sound sleep.

My next memory was of the cook and a man, who I did not know, washing me with wet rags, setting me on a bench as they changed my bed. I believe they put me back in the bed, as I spent many days in bed drifting between deep sleep and a partial wakefulness. The master came and looked at me from time to time. When I was awake, his image was fuzzy to my eyes. I had a terrible pain in my mouth and my head, which cannot be described, but I will say it was painful enough to make the oft-touted horrors of hell look less than frightening to me.

This pain and sleep continued for many days, as the new man fed me broth and honey water. He let me go to the chamber pot by helping me move there. My stomach revolted at most foods, and I had no teeth at all for a great many days, so I could not chew anything. Broth and honey water were what I drank, and from them the chamber pot was full of the most odious messes of which I had ever dreamed of in my worst nightmares.

I slept through most days and nights, being awake only for an hour at best, the rest of the time sleeping soundly in my bed. The man who attended me was present only occasionally. He would set bowls of broth and honey water out for me to feed myself. This was only a partly satisfactory solution, as it was some time before I could actually lift a bowl and feed myself. However, he was good enough to assist me in feeding myself, if he happened to be present when I was awake.

My head constantly felt like it was pounding and exploding. Saying I had a headache did not begin to describe the horrible pain. I did notice I had no hair at one point, but I was not so concerned as much as my mouth, where all of my teeth were gone. The headache slowly abated, my teeth began to return with even greater pain, and I was forced to drink milk, broth, and honey water by the gallon. The master insisted I drink full bowls of each of these several times each day. Naturally, this made my bowels open more, and my chamber pot was filled each time I was awake.

Slowly, I began waking more often and sleeping less. On one occasion, when he thought I was asleep, I heard the master tell someone he was showing me to, he was going to kill me once I was 'completely through the change.' He added he would arrange to go through this change himself, and afterwards, he would be forever young and healthy. I thought about his words and had any number of bad dreams over them. I soon decided that I would have to escape from him somehow, if I were going

IMMORTALITY

to preserve my life. I now directed myself to this goal in my few waking hours.

It was quite some time later he and the other man came and looked at me again. This time I was awake, and just beginning to eat soft foods. My teeth had come back, as had my hair, and I was actually feeling a good deal better than I pretended to be. Frankly, I was now fearful of being murdered in my sleep. My daily chamber pot was now back to a more normal odor, and my strength was returning, although I did not allow anyone to see me walking around in my room or doing those movements the teacher at the monastery had required us go through each day. I knew my strength was returning however, and I took some delight in it. On the other hand, I was deathly afraid my master might decide it was time for him to slay me. Fear made my sleep very light, and kept my mind quite wary of everything going on around me.

I counted my assets. I had three small gold coins in the box under my bed, I had checked to see they were still there. I had two changes of clothing, and an old and worn set of clothes I had set aside. I had a jacket, and I had decided I would steal a knife from the kitchen as I left. I slowly prepared myself for escape, and in a short time, I was ready to leave. To this time, I had not been seen moving about, except to weakly make my way to the chamber pot and back to my bed. I believed the master thought I was still in the midst of these strange changes, whatever they might be.

One night as I was sleeping, I awoke suddenly, smelling the smoke of a fire. I quickly gathered my things and headed for the front door, leaving without regard for the kitchen knife I had promised myself. Once in the courtyard, I saw flames coming out of the windows of the second floor rooms. I recognized them as the rooms where the master had his glass things and his furnaces. I opened the door to the path by the side of the river and stepped out. As I did, I heard a scream. The young woman who was the cook came running out of the building door into the courtyard.

A TALE OF THE ELIXIR OF LIFE

Her dress was afire, and out of instinct rather than from any knowledge, I knocked her down and rolled her on the ground until the flame was out. Her dress was now more than singed, but at least she was alive. I pointed her out to the trail, and there we went, walking downstream until we could look back to see the flames were now coming out of all of the second floor and tower rooms. The sight of the fire was quite enough for me. I continued on the way downstream in the dark, although the woman tarried, watching the fire burning in the building. I left her there and never saw her again.

I could see the trail easily in the faint light of the moon, and I wished to be far away when the fire was finally out. I was quite sure the master, and possibly the man who had cared for me, might have perished in the fire. If they had not, I was sure they would hunt me down to slay me. I walked further down the river trail until I came to a fair clearing, and there I went off deeper into the woods to find a place to sleep, as the excitement and exertion had worn me to the bone. The tiredness I felt from my exertion was a sign I was not yet as physically strong as I had thought I was. I lay my heads on my bundle of clothes and was asleep in the wink of an eye.

Morning woke me with the sound of songbirds and the dampness of dew. I realized it was now either springtime or summer. I was last conscious of the date being just past mid winter. I guessed, not being very far off at all, I had been in my bed for more than three or four months, recuperating from the single drink the doctor had given me. I was even more puzzled, as it was hard for me to conceive of losing so much time from my life to the effects of a single drink. I headed out to the clearing and found it was near the joining of the river trail with a road, which went off at an angle. I made my choice, and followed the wider road. I walked along it for quite some time, and discovered as I walked my hunger increased."

~-~

IMMORTALITY

Eventually, the man managed to establish himself as a merchant in Rome. From there, he had worked as a merchant and estate manager in various places, and, as he put it, 'had been otherwise occupied' until I met him in New York during the late 1970's. He eventually returned to Moderna, Italy, as the several Christmas cards I received from him came from there. Of course, once I stopped sending him Christmas cards, there was no further response from him.

I have no idea if his tale was true or not, but it was certainly a most interesting story. At least he confirmed some of the things I had heard from other sources concerning the critical dose of the alchemical elixir of life. To that extent, I would credit his information as being accurate.
Of course, it does open the door to all kinds of idle speculation on a variety of other subjects. ...

7

A Tale of the Wandering Jew

Having begun writing this book in my spare time, I happened to have dinner one night with my good friend Father Ambrose McGuire, SJ. Father McGuire is one of those few people I call my close friends. He is a priest who is also a magician. In the course of our conversation, I mentioned to him I was writing out some notes and stories concerning immortality and the prolongation of human life. He was interested, and asked to see the work when I was finished. Naturally, I immediately agreed he should do so.

As an item of curiosity, I asked him if he knew any stories of long-lived people. He smiled at me and said the only tale of an immortal he knew was the story of the Wandering Jew. He explained to me at various times, the church had declared there were several other immortals on the face of the earth, but he had never heard any interesting stories being told of them. I told him I had not put the story of the Wandering Jew in my notes, but I would be certain to add it to them.

I recalled a pair of writers named Viereck and Eldridge had written this story into a novel called, 'My First Two Thousand Years.' I happened to have read the book, and found it quite interesting. The story was also told in a book by Eugene

IMMORTALITY

Sue, and illustrated with a series of woodcuts by Gustave Doré. The tale of the Wandering Jew is the story of the man whom, according to one version, Christ commanded, as he was going to be crucified, to 'Tarry thou, until I come again." In the Bible, this tale is often referenced to both Matthew 16:28 and John 21:22, neither of which actually deal with any individual mentioned by Christ, and both of which have been referenced to several other people over the years.

Now as a Christian, this tale is one showing us another miracle performed by Jesus Christ, in which he commands a man to await his return, thus giving him the boon, or the curse, of immortality. As a magician, I have often wondered if this is not an example of the power of faith and belief, although according to most versions of these stories, the person Christ called to remain apparently did not believe in Christ in any manner at all. In fact, he is said to have scorned him, or even to have struck Christ, while he was on his way to be crucified.

From a magical point of view, if one believes strongly enough in the authority of someone to command them, it is possible a command given them will actually take effect, and the thing commanded will be realized. This is one of the ways in which hypnotic commands are successfully given to those who are hypnotized. The hypnotized person believes the person who hypnotizes them has the right to order them to do what they have been told to do, so they act on the command they are given without further thought. In hypnosis theory, this is called the prestige factor. This effect is a caution for those who are card and palm readers to heed; as in warning of future negative influences, they may induce someone to unknowingly bring to themselves whatever negativity the reader has told them may possibly befall them.

Those thoughts aside, the wandering Jew was supposedly either someone who was the Roman gatekeeper of Pontius Pilate, and who struck Christ as he was leaving Pilate's hall of judgment after being condemned, or he was a Jewish shoemaker who mocked and mistreated Christ, refusing him permission to

A TALE OF THE WANDERING JEW

rest, as he was making way to his crucifixion. The story states Christ tells the man he will have to wait for his second coming, leaving the man roaming the earth until judgment day.

In the original version of the story, it is more probably the individual was Roman rather than Jewish, as he was not identified as a Jew until the early seventeenth century, when anti Jewish prejudice was once again on the rise in all of Europe. The original myth, coming from the thirteenth century, seems to lend some credence to the view of the 'Wandering Jew' not really being a Jew at all, but instead being a petty Roman official, possibly even the gatekeeper of Pilate, as one version of the story suggests.

The story of the wandering Jew is quite well know in Europe, where it has a great number of regional variations. One of the more widespread of these variations says the man ages normally until he reaches a hundred years of age. At that age, he enters into a coma, and after a time is resurrected as a thirty year old, supposedly the age he was when he mistreated Christ. If so, he is certainly the only person whom this happens to, as it is quite far from any means of gaining a long life of which I have ever heard.

I hate to be a skeptic in these matters, but I sincerely doubt such a revitalization of this nature in a coma is even physiologically possible. The concept of the coma may come from the many stories of those who have taken the alchemical elixir of life. There, passage into the coma is said to be almost immediate, and the person remains in the comatose state for quite some time, although apparently waking enough each day to be fed and cared for. Usually these unfortunates release their waste where they lay, at least until their strength begins to return to them.

Some variant tales tell of the man who is supposedly the wandering Jew having been converted to Christianity, while others say, like Christ, he was born a Jew and he remains a Jew. Some other versions of the story state the wandering Jew appears when and where Jews are about to be persecuted. In this

IMMORTALITY

case, the wandering Jew apparently stands as a warning beacon to them.

As I have stated above, the earliest stories of this kind date from the thirteenth century, and are found in the works of Rodger of Wendover (in Flores Historiarum) and Matthew of Paris. Their origin seems to date from a visit by an Armenian Bishop to the monastery of St. Albans in 1228. The Bishop confirmed the truth of this tale, and named the Wanderer as Carthaphilus, (or paper lover). He added his baptismal name was Joseph, a name he took when he was converted to Christianity. The man interpreting for the Armenian bishop said the bishop knew this wanderer quite well, and had even dined with him.

Matthew of Paris states this story is true, (<u>Chron. Majora ed. Luaed</u>, London 1880, v. 340-341) and says other Armenian visitors confirmed the tale to him in 1252. Philippe Mouskes repeated the same story in his rhymed chronicles (<u>Chronicles of Phillip Mouskes</u>, ii. 491, Brussels, 1839.) of 1242, quoting the same Armenian prelate, who he says appeared in Tournai in 1243. So the story of the Wandering Jew has at least as much authenticity as many other tales of the time that are accepted as being accurate today.

In many of these early tales, the wander is not said to be Jewish. In some variants, the wanderer is said to have been a servant of Pilate, which would have made him Roman. The rabidly anti Semitic Pilate would have had no Jewish servants in his household. In other tales, the man was said to have been an officer of the Sanhedrin, the Jewish high court, which would have made him Jewish. One of the most common variants have him as a humble shoemaker, but aside from the tale of his being a servant of Pilate, the majority of the tales told in Europe say he was a Jew. To my mind, this tale of the wandering Jew is only a myth, such as are other myths of the very long-lived, including the story of Elijah. I believe if such a personage actually does, or ever did, exist, he was probably a Roman, as the earlier stories all say.

A TALE OF THE WANDERING JEW

The myth or legend of the Wandering Jew is unique in many ways, not least in the number of those people who have said they have seen him, and have reported on it. As examples: In 1505, the Wandering Jew was heard of assisting a weaver by the name of Kokot. This occurred in Bohemia, where he assisted in finding a treasure secreted by the weaver's great-grandfather sixty years earlier. Apparently, the Wandering Jew told Kokot he had been present when the treasure was hidden. According to this tale, the Wandering Jew had the appearance of a man of seventy years.

The next sighting of the Wandering Jew comes from the east, several locations near Israel or Judea, where the Wandering Jew seems to frequently have been confused with the prophet Elijah. There is no great story behind this, as it seems the Wandering Jew frequently appeared several times to both Christians and Arabians, who were fighting for possession of the Holy Land. He was particularly known to have visited some of the former crusader states, which have now been forcibly adsorbed into the nation of Israel.

In 1542, the Wandering Jew was seen in Europe, where the Reverend Paul von Eitzen, a well-known and highly respected clergyman, said he had met him in a church in Hamburg. There the wandering Jew was said to be listening attentively to the sermon. At this time, his appearance was of a man of fifty, indicating the loss of twenty years in age over the last forty some years. The pamphlet mentioned below was printed to commemorate this visitation, as well as to give proof of the crucifixion. The pamphlet was printed at the time of the Protestant reformation, when feelings ran very high on both Protestant and Catholic sides concerning any and all questions of religion.

In 1602, this pamphlet of eight pages (Ein Volksbusch) was printed in Leyden. It stated Minister Paul von Eitzen, later the Lutheran Bishop of Schleswig, had met the Wandering Jew at Hamburg in 1542, when von Eitzen was studying with Martin Luther at the University of Wittenberg. The name of the Wandering Jew, as given in the pamphlet was said to have been

IMMORTALITY

Ahasuerus. This pamphlet was dated to near the time when Luther was writing his most anti-Semitic book, 'On The Jews And Their Lies,' (Von den Jüden und ihren Lügen) which would be published in 1543. Like all of Luther's works, this book is still in print.

Ahasuerus, or the cobbler of Jerusalem, as he became known in those countries having only a slight Jewish population, (such as Norway, Sweden, and Finland) was supposed to have been a cobbler besides whose shop Jesus paused to rest while carrying his cross along the Via Dolorosa. The cobbler, probably either to impress his friends, or to curry favor with the crowd, told Jesus to leave. In reply, Jesus was reported to have said, "I will go, and quickly, but you will remain until I return."

This small eight-page pamphlet ('Kurtze Beschreibung und Erzählung von einem Juden mit Namen Ahasverus') became a best seller, going into as many as forty printings before 1700. The pamphlet, and the German myth of John Buttadaeus (John who struck God), dating from the thirteenth century, shows the myth of the Wandering Jew was both current and popular in Germany at the time. Of course, once printed, the tale spread rapidly from the literate to the illiterate of Germany by word of mouth. From Germany, the story quickly passed through all of Europe.

The myth of the wandering Jew was well known in Germany, where he was known as John Buttadaeus, while in Sicily, he was known as Buttadeu, the one who repulsed God. While visiting in Sicily, the wander was said to have introduced himself to a man named Sacalone, according to a tale reported by the daughter of Antonio Caseio, a peasant living in Salaparuta. Thomas Frederick Crane published her tale, in his book, 'Italian Popular Tales' in 1885. From the seventeenth century on, various sightings of the wandering Jew were reported from all over Europe. Until the end of the eighteenth century, the tale of the Wandering Jew, and stories of his frequent appearances were legion. In France, he was called Isaac of Old, or Lakedion, while in Spain, he was called John the Hope in God. The name

A TALE OF THE WANDERING JEW

changes, but the myth was known throughout the Christian world.

Like many other emotionally stirring and traumatic tales, the priesthood unofficially encouraged the story of the Wandering Jew in the early seventeenth century. They believed the tale of the wandering Jew encouraged belief in the immanent return of Christ, which was expected to occur in the year 1666. While the 'Wandering Jew' soon became an article of faith to the superstitious peasantry, as with all such tales, it also became another device parents used to frighten their errant children.

Between the thirteenth to the sixteenth centuries, increasing anti Semitism in Europe caused the Jews resident there to be driven out of their homes, and pushed toward the east. In part, this was because the Jews were blamed for the plague, which struck Europe with such devastating effect in the fourteenth century. In 1290, the Jews were driven out of England. Between 1306 and 1394, they were driven from France. In 1400, Jews were forcibly driven from Prague, while in 1492; they were forced to leave Spain. This last exodus happened on the 9th of Ab, historically the day of the destruction of the Temple by the Romans. In following year, 1493, Jews were banished from Austria and the Austrian empire. By 1520, Jews had been banished from almost all of Europe. During all this time, the story of the Wandering Jew was widely circulated in Europe, even before it was first published in 1602. Of course, once the pamphlet was printed, the tale flared into life and became far more popular. In the mid 1600's, the story of the wandering Jew was being taught to children at their parent's knees as if it were part of the gospel.

Both Martin Luther and Philipp Melanchton (1497 - 1560) accepted the story of the wandering Jew as being valid, although I wonder if they really believed it to be true. In those superstitious times, they may well have completely accepted it. The story was certainly a good morality tale. It was used as such for many years all through Europe. The story of the homeless wanderer occasionally appears in sermons even today.

IMMORTALITY

For someone who was only a myth, there were a great many reports of those who said they had seen him. In 1547, he was sighted in Hamburg, in 1575, in Spain. In 1599, he was seen in Vienna, while 1601 found him in Lübeck, and the following year he was in Prague, returning to Lübeck in 1603.

In 1604, the Wandering Jew was said to be in both Bavaria and Paris, later he was reported to be in Spain, Italy, and Germany. In 1623, he was sighted in Ypres. In 1633, he was reported in Hamburg, while in 1640, he was seen in Brussels. He was reportedly in Leipzig in 1642, seen at Paris in 1644, found in Skara Sweden in 1652, Stamford in 1658. He was in Astrakhan in 1672, and encountered at the Castle Frankenstein in Germany in 1676. In the same year he was seen at Zabkowice Slaskie, while in 1684, he was seen in Stuttgart.

In the beginning of the eighteenth century, it was reported he was interviewed in London, but it seems he had vanished into Sweden a few years later. He was seen before the gates of Munich on the 22d of July 1721, interviewed at Altbach in 1766, found in Brussels in 1774, and met in Newcastle England in 1790. He was certainly well traveled, I wonder at his traveling expenses. They must have been considerable.

Sometime in the first half of the nineteenth century, Frau Bandow from Fünfeichen, Germany said she met him, and even gave him a piece of her bread. She repeated the story to her neighbors, being proud she had met this human oddity. When she was eighty-one years old, her tale was collected and published by Karl Gander as a folk tale, in 1894. She said she had discussed the incident with the preacher of her church at the time and he had confirmed it was probably the 'Lost Jew,' a regional name for the wandering Jew.

Because the tale of the wandering Jew was a popular one, it became an element in literature, if it were not the focus of the story. Appearing frequently in both poems and novels, he has also been found in comic books and films. Shelley's Queen Mab and other tales use the wandering Jew as a character, while in Eugene Sue's 'Wandering Jew,' and the novel 'My First Two

A TALE OF THE WANDERING JEW

Thousand Years,' the wanderer takes center stage himself. Of course, the tale of the Wandering Jew has now been popularized in both speech and literature. There are several dozen books concerning his supposed adventures.

By the early nineteenth century, it seems the living Wandering Jew appears no more. Such sightings as were reported after about 1850 were usually attributed to the desires of fools and the delusions of madmen. His appearances all over Europe, and even in the depths of Russia, ceased, and thus his story is no longer as well known in superstition and folklore as it formerly was. This decline, beginning in the nineteenth century, lasts into the twentieth, and twenty-first centuries. This despite the reported appearance of the Wandering Jew to a Mormon named O'Grady in Salt Lake City in 1868 (Desert News, Sept 23d, 1868). However, the usefulness of the Wandering Jew as a fictional character is undoubted. In the early nineteenth century, Nathaniel Hawthorne supposedly wrote of him in a far earthier vein (although I could not find any citation of him in Hawthorne's collected works).

By the mid twentieth century, the tale of the Wandering Jew became the subject of the research scholar, and today he has become the subject of numerous academic books. Soren Kirkegaard even thought the myth of the Wandering Jew was one of the fundamental myths of Europe, along with the story of the famous Dr. Faust.

The original Dr. Faust was a real person, who lived about 1350. He was nothing at all like the tale told of him by Goethe. His supposed life's story was first told in the 'Historia von D. Johann Fausten' published at Frankfurt am Main, by Johann Spies in 1587. This book painted Faust as a prankster and player of odd and silly deeds, who died in repentant agony, having sold his soul to the devil. However, there is no valid record the real Fausten ever sold his soul to the devil, lusted after young maidens, or did anything at all like Goethe or others ever credited Faust with. Nor was Herr Fausten ever known to have dealt with Satan, or with evil in any way.

IMMORTALITY

I believe Jung gave the story of the Wandering Jew some credence in his psychoanalytic theories as well. The books of scholars now trace the story of the Wandering Jew, its many regional variations, and its frequent developments.

I still believe it is based entirely on a myth, and is not a real tale at all. But who knows? There are certainly stranger things in this world than a very long-lived man awaiting the return of Christ. Certainly many living Christians eagerly await the return of Christ with the same hope and expectation Christians have used in their recorded strivings for this event since before 40 AD.

Other Immortals

Every people and nation has tales and stories of living immortals. The Greeks had the story of Aristeas; a poet whom they said had appeared among the various peoples of the world off and on for well over four hundred years.

Pope Innocent III pointed out in his 1208 bull, 'God made Cain a wanderer and a fugitive on the earth.' Thus, in Christian Theology, Cain is said to wander the earth forever repenting the killing of his brother Able. It is said God marked him so he could not be slain. This is another version of God granted immortality.

Malchus, whose ear St. Peter cut off in the garden of Gethsemane (John 18:10) was also said to have been condemned to wander the earth until the second coming. Another tale has him being eternally punished with the curse of immortality for striking the Madonna. Still another tale of Malchus has him living in a hollow under a mountain, condemned to walk around a column until the end of the world frees him from this monotonous task. He is said to have worn so deep a crevice around the column now, he walks with only his head showing above the floor. According to one version of the Malchus myth, for the

IMMORTALITY

seven years before the world ends, there will be no children born anywhere on earth.

Joseph of Arimathea was also said to have had his life preserved by Jesus, but his immortality was granted him as a blessing, rather than as a curse. Because of this blessing granted him by Jesus, he was placed among those who supposedly live forever.

Apollonius of Tyana, a contemporary of Jesus Christ, was another who was said to have become an immortal. He was born at Tyana in 4 BC, but there is no record of his death, although many of the various achievements of his rather interesting life have been well documented. He was widely traveled in the Mediterranean, and at least one author - Robert Graves in 'King Jesus' - claimed Apollonius knew Jesus Christ, and even worked with him. Apollonius was last seen in Ephesus about 100 AD. I know of no further reports of his being seen, either alive or dead.

Jesus Christ supposedly taught physical immortality. It was claimed he taught the physical resurrection of the bodies of those who were dead would occur at the end of the world. The truth of Christ actually having taught this is subject to debate by some theologians.

Aside from those who are actively living forever on the earth, similar tales are told of sleeping kings and heroes of old, who patiently wait for their resurrection so they may come to the aid of their nation in time of need. In this class of immortals are found both King Arthur, and Frederick Barbarossa.

Rip Van Winkle and Thomas the Rhymer were supposedly granted greatly extended lives by their sleeping in trance for years or even decades according to their legends.

Enoch is one of the earliest of the physical immortals. He is mentioned as walking with God in the book of Genesis (Gen. 5:24) in the Old Testament of the Bible.

The prophet Elijah is also credited with having been granted physical immortality by God in 2d Kings 2: 1-11. Again, as in the case of other figures of antiquity, the grant was given to them as a boon, not as a curse. The Passover meal has a cup set aside for Elijah, should he care to join the table, something well known even among non Jews. Devout Jews believe he is able to walk through the door and sit at the table, participating with the family in the Passover feast. A cabalistic magical ritual, which is designed to summon Elijah, exists, although I have no idea if it has ever been successfully used for the intended purpose.

The Mormons have the three Nephites, said to be three immortals that wander about the western hemispheres doing good works and prophesying. They have supposedly been active at this for two thousand years. Unlike the Wandering Jew, whose longevity is due to a curse from Christ, the three Nephites enjoy both freedom from death and eternal youth, because they have received both eternal life and their commission to preach and prophesy directly from God, as a divine blessing.

In the Gilgamesh myth, Utnapishtim and his wife were granted immortality following the great flood. If they still live in Iran, they are likely to be the best-known immortals of the Middle East.

In China, the eight Immortals of Tao mythology were also granted a long if not an eternal life. Four of them are known historical figures. Known as the Ba Xian, they are said to give instruction to the worthy and assistance to the needy. Their names and figures are found in Chinese art and literature.

Some of the Chinese emperors sought immortality by taking alchemical draughts made of cinnabar, the red Mercuric Oxide. As cinnabar is toxic in itself, and as the ore often contains toxic arsenic, the results were the opposite of the emperor's expectations. Three emperors of China are known to have died from alchemical mixtures their court alchemists supplied them, supposedly as life-enhancing potents. It is quite likely several other emperors met their fate in this manner.

Other immortals are known to come from Asia, some of whom live on an invisible island Penglai Shan, on the east coast

IMMORTALITY

of China. The eight Taoist immortals are said to live here among their contemporaries, in dwellings of silver and gold.

In England, the perfect knight of King Arthur's round table, Sir Galahad, was said to have earned immortality both through his personal virtue and his discovery of the Holy Grail. Merlin, the magician of the King Arthur saga also attained immortality of a sort, being sealed up in a cave by the young woman he loved, and to whom he taught the secrets of his magic. It is presumed that through use of his magical arts, Merlin is still alive.

One of the most famous couples who immortality is claimed for are Nicholas and Perenelle Flamel. Nicolas Flamel was known to be an alchemist in Paris during the fourteenth century. Contemporary documents exist, attesting to details of his life and his many charities. Supposedly, he and his wife acquired eternal life through the practice of alchemy. Reports of his being seen in both Turkey and India over the years have contributed to this tale.

The eccentric physician Paracelsus, who contributed so much to cast off the dead hand of the ancients from medical practice and improved the medical knowledge of the time, is occasionally considered another physical immortal. This despite the story he died on September 24th, 1541, and was buried in the churchyard of St Sebastian in Salzburg. The existence of a tomb where he is supposedly buried has proved to be no barrier to those who claim he is an immortal, and lives among us to this day.

One of the more recent, and possibly the most famous supposed immortal is the Count de St. Germain. Despite his death, which was witnessed by a physician on February 27th 1784, he developed the reputation as an immortal in his lifetime. The fact that his enemies at the court of Louis XV cast this reputation upon him as an aspersion has not dimmed the fervor of those who wish to see him as an imortal. Although this reputation has followed the mysterious Count down the years, the only statement the count is known to have ever made concerning his

OTHER IMMORTALS

age was, 'he had been told he did not look to be as old as he was.' Many of us have probably said that at various times of our life. Despite his not claiming great age, he was given the reputation of being many centuries old by those who desired to create strife between him and the French king. This reputation clings to him today, as various occult and religious organizations have claimed him as either being alive, and either guiding them from the spirit world, or as being one of their 'ascended masters.' I believe the count, if he actually were alive, would find these various claims to be quite humorous.

In addition to these supposed immortals, there are several cases of caskets being opened, and the investigators finding them empty. This often gives rise to the tale the person supposedly buried in the grave was actually an immortal. Aside from the logs said to have replaced the bodies of the Flamel's, the headless body of Vald the Impaler, considered the model for the vampire Dracula, was found to be missing from his burial place, when the church in which he was buried was undergoing renovations. Could he have joined the physical immortals? An immortal Dracula is a scary thought.

Then there is the tale that the body of Czar Ivan the Terrible was missing from his grave. Another frightening image, at least to my mind.

The casket of Czar Alexander, who defeated Napoleon in his invasion of Russia, was opened in 1926. The casket was found to be empty. According to his biography, Czar Alexander was certainly scheming and cunning enough to have arranged his own funeral to gain some political advantage. Could he have become another immortal? This certainly seems unlikely, but who knows the truth about such things? Rumor always flies on well-viewed wings, while truth shuffles along unheeded.

I know at least one man who believes immortals walk among us every day. He is a sober fellow, and I trust his judgment in many other matters. His unquestioned belief in the physical immortality of a few people occasionally gives me pause, although personally, I find it very difficult to accept.

IMMORTALITY

Processes of Immortality

The process of non-physically transferring oneself from a dying body to a new host body is the process used in two of these stories, those of Betty and Gloria and Varmus. This technique could be considered a more complete means of astral projection than what is normally practiced or ever ordinarily encountered. I believe the use of this technique might be a real possibility for anyone who could first master successfully consciously projecting themselves out of their physical body, mastering navigating in the physical world, and gradually develop the art of projection of their non-physical being even further than it is ordinarily extended.

One of the several reasons I believe this method might possibly be a valid one is there are a great number of stories of Indian Yogis who are said to have practiced 'body jumping,' passing from their body to another, and thereby being recognized as living greatly extended lives. There are frequent recurrences of this idea, in both fables and tales, so such a method of gaining a kind of immortality cannot be dismissed outright. Those of us who have projected out of our physical body into the physical world are well aware further projection is possible, however it has always seemed to me to be potentially

IMMORTALITY

life threatening. Thus, there are tales of the 'silver cord,' connecting the projector to the projection, which must not be severed on pain of death.

I understand the well-known Czechoslovakian magician Frantz Bardon practiced an annual projection of his non-physical body, either of this kind, or of one of a rather similar nature. He supposedly stated if he were to be interrupted in this projection, it would cause his immediate physical death. It might be this kind of complete projection of the non-physical system from the physical body is not so rare as I would have believed it to be. There is some slight information in Bardon's books concerning this kind of projection of the non-physical body.

The ability to project the non-physical body from the physical body is more common than might be supposed, although it usually takes devoting some serious time and effort to develop sufficient expertise with the art to claim mastery of the technique of non-physical projection. Usually, the ability to project the non-physical body is both natural and sporadic, and as such, it is never fully controlled by the person who discovers they project involuntarily. Obviously, for those who wish to use this method of gaining immortality, it is necessary to first master the conscious and controlled projection of their non-physical body into the physical world. I have given some information concerning mastering this art in my book, '<u>Magic Simplified</u>.' I will state that it requires much work and mental concentration to master. Several other texts also cover the art of astral projection.

Projection of the non physical body into the non-physical realms leaves the person open to the delusion of success so pleasing to those who wish to either visit these realms for entertainment, or who desire to find simple solutions to the complex problems of life on the earth. It would serve no good purpose for someone who actually sought physical immortality to involve themselves in this pleasing delusion. The serious student must master projection of their non-physical body into the physical world. Projection into the non-physical world is often confused with what is known as lucid dreaming.

The additional exercises an individual who can project out of their physical body into the physical world must master to attain the goal of being able to transfer their nonphysical being to a new physical vessel on death are those making the projection of the many components of the non-physical form from the physical body complete. Once the basic principles of projection of the non physical body are mastered, the person who wishes to maintain immortality in this way must continue practicing these projections, always drawing more and more of their essential self into the non-physical form they project from their physical body. As the person ages and gains experience, more and more of their non physical essence may be projected, although until the death of the person's physical body is actually at hand, there will always remain some increasingly smaller vital essence connecting them to their physical body.

Of course, for someone who has experience projecting out of their physical body, the process of having their own body die on their command is simplicity itself. Thus, the projector has the opportunity of avoiding long suffering illnesses, by dying when the terminal nature of their physical difficulty is made apparent to them. They also can allow themselves to die in a situation in which they can best locate a satisfactory new body to inhabit.

Once the physical body of the person desiring immortality perishes, on their command or otherwise, the person is now able to project all of their non-physical essence into their non-physical form. Speed is now important, as they must connect themselves with someone in a physical body as quickly as possible. This must be done to either to enter into the body, supplanting the normal non-physical self of the chosen victim, or to draw vital energy from the person, in a vampiric manner, while directing them mentally to go where the proposed immortal can find someone they might wish to enter into. It would seem a suitable victim must be located rapidly, probably within an hour or less of the death of their former physical body. Failing this, they will be forced to fully occupy the body with which they first joined themselves with, in what is actually a kind of vampiric communion.

Naturally, having a receptacle for a future life designated in advance makes it considerably easier, so long as the dying person is physically close to their chosen receptacle at the very moment of death. Once the non-physical essence of the person has fully entered into a new body, it will have to remain there until it is time for the death of their 'new' physical body. Of course, the person desiring immortality will also have to once again master the exercises allowing it to project more and more of its non-physical self out of its physical body.

It should be obvious there is going to be a struggle between the two personalities occupying the 'new' physical body, the personality of the natural occupant, and the personality of the invader. There have been several such personality struggles reported in the literature of abnormal psychology, as may be found in the case of some of those with traumatic multiple personality disorder. Psychology professionals not usually being equipped with the sight, it is unknown if there were actually two contrasting personalities fighting for survival within the human shell, or if there was only one, which was greatly disturbed for some reason. It may be at least some of these cases of traumatic multiple personality disorder are actually cases of forced possession by another, quite possibly by a recently deceased, human being. Who knows?

It would be interesting to see if, following the 'cure' of the person with multiple personality disorder, their life took an unusual turn, one not characteristic of them in their former existence. Any new inhabitant of a body will quite naturally wish to maintain at least some of its former habits, and these changing habits might possibly indicate there has been a change in the control and ownership of the physical body involved.

In a number of instances, similar changes in personality, as well as alterations in both desires and behavior, have been reportedly found among those who have undergone successful organ transplants. This poses the question as to whether part or most of the non-physical body from which the organ was taken has accompanied the organ to the new host. It is quite possible this could actually happen. It would be interesting to have someone who was trained in the non-physical realms look at a few of these interesting people. I doubt that modern science would accept this explanation, as it is to far from the safe realm of their physical knowledge.

To my mind, this influx of the new personality is just one among many other reasons why organ transplants are not ever a good idea, either for the donor or the recipient. I know the idea of transplants is a popular one, but my objections to the process are rooted in this difficulty. My objections to this procedure also include several other more esoteric considerations.

The association of someone having these abilities of non-physical projection along with a strong and focused mind, one capable of commanding and controlling others, and even of draining their life's energy from them, is not automatic. The mental body must also be trained over the years, but if non-physical projection training were being accomplished, it would seem the additional mental training required to master concentration and visualization would not be particularly burdensome to those who might seriously wish to engage in prolonging their life. The inducement of immortality might be a sufficient stimulus for the interested person to undergo this initially quite difficult mental and projection training.

Interestingly enough, the mental training is easier to renew in a new body than is the ability to project oneself completely out of the physical body. This is because the training and discipline of the mental self is essentially a one-time affair, which may usually be carried forward from one life into another. Naturally, the skill is usually renewed and improved with practice. However, mastery of projection of the non-physical body involves both non-physical and physical processes, and therefore it must be mastered anew with each incarnation, or with each new physical body occupied by the non-physical entity. Such mastery takes at least some time, it is not automatic.

IMMORTALITY

The process of drawing energy from food best illustrates the process of drawing the non-physical or vital energy from another person. Should you happen to be fasting, and having missed at least one of your ordinary meals, look intently at something you would ordinarily wish to eat. Now as you inhale a breath, visualize yourself drawing the non-physical energy from the food into yourself. Hold the breath, allowing the energy of the food to be received within you. Now exhale normally. Repeat this process several times until you feel you have drained all of the energy from the food you have been looking at. If you practice this before each meal, or whenever you are cooking a meal, you will find you can usually grasp the technique without difficulty.

You will have mastered this process when you find you can, in a week of otherwise eating normal meals, fast completely for between a day to three days, or in time, fast even longer, and yet not lose any of your vital energy. You will maintain your energy because you have taken the energy from the meals you either observed or cooked. You have drained the non-physical energy from the food, although you did not physically eat any of it. Once you have attained this goal, you need now just inhale the vital energy from such foods, as you may find on display in supermarkets, or any other stores you might visit in your daily life. This is a worthwhile technique for those who wish to control their weight to master, as well as for those who wish to master this useful art for other reasons. Those people who regularly fast for a week or more at a time are often among those who have learned this technique, either consciously and deliberately, or otherwise.

As with all other things in human life, the conscious practice of this, or any other art, either occult or worldly, is always to be preferred to using the same art unconsciously. Mastering the art of consciously living your life is what gains you merit in the world. You should do what you can to be conscious of everything you do, whether it is a magical or occult act, or dealing with the mundane tasks of your daily life.

A similar technique is praying over an alcoholic beverage for the alcoholic content of the beverage to be dissipated, and not affect you as you drink the beverage. This is more effective with practice, but if you drink with others for whatever reason, it is a technique I believe is certainly worth trying to master.

Incidentally, as far as I know, this is not at all the same practice, as those people of whom I have read who supposedly do not eat at all. I believe they are in a different category altogether, as when performing the exercise given above, you will still need to eat from time to time, although the amount of food you consume will usually radically decrease, while you continue to maintain your previous level of energy. This is not a diet plan, nor is it a means of regulating your weight. It is only a method for maintaining the non-physical energy powering your existence without eating the regular amount of food.

I would make a very poor academic, as while I have read widely in the past, I have seldom noted or recalled where I read these various tidbits and facts so often seeming to fill my mind to overflowing. I do recall reading a book in which a mother advised her daughter about 'borrowing energy' from other people. I have no idea if this information was found in a novel, which I read for recreation, or in an occult text.

The process the mother taught her daughter was to ask, consciously or sub consciously, to 'borrow,' or to 'use,' the energy of the other person. Once agreement was reached, as it usually is quickly reached when requested subconsciously, the energy of the other person was made available to the borrower. This is an example of the kind of mental power exhibited by the retired army physician in, 'Betty and Gloria.' Two other examples from my own experience follow.

Many years ago, a man came to me for a consultation, as he was sure his wife and another man were attempting to curse him, causing his death. Ordinarily he was only very rarely sick, yet he had been ill, and away from his work for the last three weeks. I did a reading on this man's difficulty, and found he was

IMMORTALITY

correct. A serious and a very strong effort was being made to kill him with a curse. Through his knowledge of the situation, I also discovered which of three possible men he had in mind were attempting to plot his demise. The perpetrator of these curses was one of the three men he had suspected of having a carnal interest in his attractive wife.

Once the situation was understood, and the players in this drama identified, the man told me quite confidently he could handle the problem himself. He had only needed to obtain outside confirmation of the presence of the curse, and identify the person or person's who were actively cursing him. I was about to offer to break the curse and make a protective charm for the man when he told me this.

The man took a packet of photographs out of his pocket. He selected the photograph of the man we had identified as being behind the plot, and sitting at my consultation table, he concentrated upon the man, and, as he told me later, he began draining the life energy from him. He worked at this for about fifteen minutes and replaced the photograph in his pocket. Turning to me with a smile, he said he had solved the problem. He paid me for my time, the reading I had given him, and he left.

The following day the newspaper delivered to my apartment door had a twin. The additional copy was folded open, and a small notice on the bottom of an inside page was boldly circled with a crayon. The circled notice told of the death of the man who had been identified as the culprit. The one who was attempting to murder my client psychically had passed on. According to the notice in the newspaper, the man had collapsed at work, and had suddenly died of what was apparently a massive heart attacked. This idea gave me real pause, as while I had heard such a thing could be accomplished, I had never before seen an example of it.

I carefully reviewed the reading I had given the man and its aftermath in my mind. I eventually concluded the man had concentrated himself strongly on the photograph, and had literally sucked the vital energy out of the man who had been identified as his enemy. Furthermore, he had accomplished this feat as he sat right in front of me. To say I was amazed at seeing this would be an understatement. It was certainly my first, and actually my only experience with such a thing. I still have some lingering doubts this was what the man actually did, he only said he took energy form him, but I really have no other explanation for this happening.

~

As far as placing ideas firmly into the mind of another, to gain your desires, is concerned, I met with an excellent example of this talent from what I considered a most unusual source. During the Second World War, one of the other tenants of the apartment building I lived in had a relative who was serving in the Italian Army. She was an elderly woman who only rarely left her apartment. One day I had cause to call on her, and knocked at her door. As there was no answer, I assumed she was out, either shopping or at church, her two usual destinations. I went on my way, and on my return found her waiting for me in the hallway. I told her I had knocked earlier, and she invited me into her apartment.

She informed me she was busy making sure her relative came to America, as he had recently been taken a prisoner of war in North Africa. Naturally, I smiled on hearing her words. This grandmotherly looking lady did not seem to me to have the ability to do anything nearly as spectacular.

However, over a cup of coffee, she explained to me exactly how she did it, holding nothing at all back. I was amazed. Not only was this kindly old grandmother a conscious astral projector, she was able to drive ideas into the minds of others with such force, and to such strong effect, they quickly agreed with whatever she wished them to do. I was truly surprised to discover this very rare talent in her. For my part, I had been trying for many years to develop this same ability within myself, but without having nearly the same success she had so easily demonstrated to me.

IMMORTALITY

Four months later, her relative, released on parole from Governors Island where he was employed as a groundskeeper, visited the old lady on a Sunday. She invited me down to her apartment for a celebratory dinner, and I met the man. Of all of the thousands of Italian Army prisoners, he alone had been selected to come to New York City, to work as a groundskeeper at Governors Island. For the rest of the war, he had Sundays off, to spend with his 'New York family.' I doubted many of the other Italian prisoners of war residing in America had this kind of advantage granted them.

I am reasonably sure this kindly old Italian lady could have performed all of the mental fetes attributed to the retired army doctor in the tale of Betty and Gloria. I was also quite glad we had been friends ever since I had moved into the building. Her abilities in accomplishing those kinds of mental tasks, dominating and controlling the thoughts of others, certainly far surpassed my own poor efforts in that area. I was quite happy to learn from her whatever she was willing to teach me.

Alchemy and the Elixir of Life

The Alchemical 'Elixir of Life' is featured in the other two tales in this book. This elixir is always the product of the alchemist art, but none of the few alchemists I have ever known either knew how to make it, or claimed to be the least bit interested in searching for it. Instead, the alchemists of my acquaintance make alchemical alcohol, and any number of salves, unguents, and medications used in healing the physical and the non-physical body of man. Of course, they use their slight income from this work to research in other areas, but none of these areas seem to touch on eternal life. Most alchemists seem to be quite satisfied with the three score and ten years or so of life granted them by their creator. Alchemy is at least as far from my field of knowledge as Musicology, of which I know nothing at all. Thus, should this also be the case with you, I add here some slight introductory notes concerning my slight acquaintance with the history of this strange non-physical art.

The study of alchemy supposedly began in the Middle East about 410 AD. However, there is good reason to suspect the study of alchemy actually originated in the orient at a considerably earlier date. There is a long tradition of making both gold and immortals, by alchemists in both China and India. These traditions predate the time of its supposed origin in the Middle East.

Originally, the study of alchemy was directed toward the dual goals of conversion of ordinary metals to gold, and the search for the elixir of life, or the universal medicine. This reveals the two branches of Alchemy, herbal alchemy used to make medicines of various kinds, and metallic alchemy, used in the transmutation of metals. These metals apparently are not always transmuted to gold or silver. I understand there is a Chinese book concerning sword-making alchemy.

Alchemy came to Europe much later, publicly appearing at a demonstration at Toledo, in Moorish Spain, on February 11th, 1144. There alchemy soon became a more directed search for gold, and only secondarily, was used either in the search for health or longevity. It was said at the time that alchemists in the Middle East, men of evolved character, and unquestioned spirituality, were involved in making gold for the courts of the Saracens. Naturally, the rulers of Europe hoped for this same boon, so in a few years the search for gold by both serious alchemists, as well as by a large and colorful variety of frauds and confidence men, was well underway.

Until the Spanish began bringing gold as treasure from the new world, during the 1500's, precious metals, especially gold, were in woefully short supply in all of Europe. The alchemist who could produce gold was welcome, and those who traveled Europe saying they could make gold were given the opportunity to prove themselves by cash strapped and gold hungry royalty. Unfortunately, very few of these pretenders actually made gold, while a many of them wasted the funds of various kings and noblemen in a vain search for a way to make the metal.

IMMORTALITY

Rudolph the King of Bohemia, had a street near his palace in Prague, still known as the 'Street of the Puffers,' where alchemists vainly attempted to make gold to fill his purse. However, apparently some alchemical gold was actually being made there. There are stories of some minor successes, but there was never enough gold being made to please Rudolph. Edward Kelly, the associate of Dr. John Dee, supposedly made some gold for King Rudolph.

The appointment of Isaac Newton as the master of the mint in England immediately resulted in the minting of British gold 'rose nobles.' There was considerable suspicion the gold from which these coins were minted had been made alchemically, by Newton working in his laboratory in the Tower of London. I have been told the source of the gold used to mint these coins is actually unknown. It makes an interesting story if nothing else.

Should anyone doubt the making of gold from base metal was actually a possibility, there are any number of written testimonies by well-regarded men of the time who said they had seen the process carried out in their presence. Of course, physical scientists today are convinced all of these affairs were frauds.

It is quite likely, there were alchemists making gold in the Far and Middle East at one time. The alchemical art is no stranger to either India or China, as alchemy, and the process of transmutation of both vegetable and mineral substances has been known in both places for a very long time. There are a large number of Chinese books on the alchemical art, some of which are said to be far more plain spoken than those written when the Roman Catholic Church and its Holy Inquisition were controlling men's thoughts and minds during the Middle Ages in Europe.

The fabled Elixir of Life was a different matter altogether. It always seemed to take second place, or an even lesser position to the frantic European search for gold. As found in fiction, according to the story of one author, James Cowan, the elixir of life comes from the mutual death of elephants and dragons, and is found in cinnabar, the poisonous red mercuric oxide. To Honore de Balzac, it was the essence of the exudent of a rock in the wilderness, perhaps the very rock struck by Moses to gain water for the Israelites in the desert. Both tales are purely fictions, although a part of the many pleasant stories told by these well-known authors. Most writers mentioning the elixir do not go so far as to try to identify how it is made. Some say it is noxious, others that it is cordial like. I doubt any of these writers have ever seen it.

According to a friend of mine, an alchemist of many years standing, the powder used to changes base metals into gold is of much the same color as cinnabar, but is of a different composition all together. Other authorities verify the color of this powder as being like the color of cinnabar, a brownish red, or reddish brown. However, I have heard no one tell me of the color of the elixir of life. My guess would be it is reddish in color and somewhat viscous, like a good thick fruit cordial. All of my alchemist friends say they have not made it, and they have no interest in doing so. On the other hand, it is always described as a liquid, while the material used to change common metals into gold is always described as either a solid mineral substance, or a powder. Could this be a clue for the knowing? Perhaps something here is worth investigating further.

As the alchemists of the middle ages searched for ways to make gold, they also discovered a number of healing modalities used in both natural and folk medicine today. One of these was the power of dew, which we find is used today in the Bach Remedies, as well as in other varieties of Flower Essences. These essences are used in treating and relieving psychological conditions, and their associated physical complaints. Another alchemical discovery was the idea of gem and metal essences, which may be used less often today, but are still found useful in treating some physical and non-physical conditions, particularly in India among Ayurvedic physicians. Both of these medicines have been used in the Far East for many centuries. Their value was probably also revealed there by alchemists. Paracelsus was known to have written on both of these rather rarely used healing modalities.

As one of the known positive results of the European and Middle Eastern craze for alchemy, much of the equipment and processes found and used in the chemical laboratory today, as well as many laboratory techniques and chemical discoveries, originated in the workrooms of alchemists. A French female alchemist named Marie invented the Bain Marie or the water bath. Cooks use its cousin today, the double boiler. Arabian alchemists originally discovered the process of distillation, as they also discovered techniques and procedures perfecting the art of fermentation, the process used in making beer, wine, and a number of modern anti bacterial drugs, among a great many other things. Arabian alchemists perfected the distillation apparatus, although the process has gone through great development, it has had but few fundamental changes since that time.

Alcohol

Once the Arabs distilled alcohol, in about the turn of the tenth century, it was quickly assumed it was the elixir of life. Thus, we have names for alcoholic beverages today indicating this early belief. Aqua Vita, or water of life, and Whiskey (from the Gaelic visce beathadh water of life), are examples of these names applied to distilled alcoholic beverages. Both Jabir ibn Hayyan in the eighth century and Al Rahzi in the ninth century expressed the belief alcohol was a life giving elixir. Alchemists and others considered the burning of water clear alcohol to be something of great interest. Naturally, the burning water like liquid alcohol led to the liquid being given the name 'firewater,' by Native Americans among many other people. Naturally, the flammability of alcohol was used in military tactics almost immediately after its discovery. Should you wonder how, think of shooting flaming arrows at the enemy.

However, making strong drink aside, there was no chance drinking alcohol would extend human life, something quickly discovered by those desiring to extend their lives through drinking heavily. Turning from alcoholic beverages, the search for the elusive elixir of life continued.

Paracelsus, the controversial physician and alchemist of the sixteenth century developed and expanded theories of 'healing dews, gem and metal essences,' as well as many other procedures derived from the alchemists of his day. He was the first to insist both inorganic and organic chemicals had a place in medicine as healing agents. He introduced Opium, Ammonia, and several dozen other chemicals to the practice of medicine. As far as anyone knows, Paracelsus was not successful in either discovering the elixir of life, or in making gold. However, he said of the Philosopher's Stone, which is used to make gold as well as supposedly to make the elixir of life:

> The Philosopher's Stone purges the whole body of man, and cleanses it from all impurities by the introduction of new and more youthful forces, which it joins to the nature of man. (Fifth Book of the Archidoxies, quoted on page 35 of 'Alchemy Ancient and Modern,' By H. Stanley Redgrove.

Apparently, Paracelsus did not believe in the possibility of physical immortality, although he was quite interested in defeating illness and prolonging life. Since the sixteenth century, various factions have promoted many versions of the elixir of life and its far less dramatic tonic variations. One of these tonics, a blend supposedly developed by Paracelsus, is sold today as 'Maria Treben's Authentic Swedish Bitters.' I have tried this tonic, and while I recommend it as a useful tonic, I can testify from my own experience that it does not reduce the effects of aging, nor does it promote a youthful appearance, neither of which effects are claimed for it by the manufacturer. Having taken it for a year or more, I may say it was a good tonic, but it did nothing for my increasing age and physical debility. However, I do believe I was slightly more energized from taking it.

IMMORTALITY

My alchemist friends have told me there are supposedly either ten or twelve ingredients in the composition of the supposed elixir of life. Knowing the philosophy of their subject better than I, they believe there are more likely to be twelve ingredients than ten, as twelve suits the nature of the alchemical process, which is a mystical art, if it is nothing else. Apparently, a there is fictional story concerning making the elixir, which had its hero searching the world for the ten life giving ingredients, only to eventually find them growing in a hedgerow near his home.

Two of the herbs comprising the elixir of life are said to be lemon grass and wheat grass. They are supposed to be disassembled alchemically, separated into their constituent parts, their alchemical sulfur, salt, and mercury, and mixed together again, forming a new compound with very different properties from the old. I have no idea what the other constituents of the so-called elixir of life might be, and neither do any of the alchemists I have discussed this with.

The Chinese herb He Shou Wu or Fo Ti is also known as the elixir of life, as it has the reputation of extending the life of those who consume it in their diet. In fact, it is often used to reduce the presence of gray hair, found on the head of older people, although I have tried it and found it did little for my own gray head. Perhaps I did not use it for a long enough time. This herb is also prescribed as a tonic for women going through menopause.

The plant grows as a crawling vine, having no restrictions, but usually covering about thirty feet of fencing to a height of four or five feet or more. As an ornamental plant, it is a better choice than many others, its multiple cream covered flowers making it look as if it were a sheep fleece draped upon the fence on which it grows. The Botanical name is Polygonum Multiflorum, and it is frequently recommended both as a domestic decorative vine and as a culinary herb in ordinary cooking. Of course, the Chinese also use it as a medicinal.

Other plants have similar reputations as healing agents, for example there is a lovely purple flower known as 'All Heal.' An extract of this flower was once said to cure all diseases. Many years ago, when I was more daring and experimental with my more vigorous health, a well-meaning friend made up the extract and seemingly used it satisfactorily upon himself for quite some time. When I had a slight cold, he gave me some of the extract in a tea. Unfortunately, I had a most severe reaction to it. I supposed one might say it caused a purge of my system, but the results of the single dose were far less comfortable to me than the rather uncomfortable cold had been. Now I approach all healing efforts not coming from my physician with a great deal more suspicion.

Valerian, Valerian Officinalis, is also known as All Heal, according to my copy of the most useful, 'J. M. Nickell's Botanical Ready Reference.' It may be it was this herb my well-meaning friend gave me in a tea. The herb is known as a tonic and is useful in calming the nerves, as is Chamomile. I have never heard it seriously mentioned in connection with the alchemical elixir of life however. I suppose that other herbs must be looked at to find the constituents of that very rare alchemical marvel.

Science And The Search For A Long Life

According to the researches of modern science, polyphenols, such as resveratrol, found in red wine, are said to promote long life. Those who have read the New Testament may recall St Paul's statement about a glass of wine being good for the stomach (I Timothy 5:23). Apparently, researchers have discovered these resveratrols can increase the length of life of yeasts, flies, and worms. Experiments are continuing to learn if they can increase the life span of mice and other small animals. Eventually, there will be a further investigation to see if they can increase the lifespan of larger animals, and quite probably, these products of the vintner will eventually be investigated for their effect on humans.

IMMORTALITY

Another means of gaining a long life is reducing the consumption of foods. Those who eat a balanced diet, but a smaller quantity of food, usually live longer than those who indulge themselves, and especially those who are obese. As might be expected, those with chronic diseases such as diabetes, high blood pressure, or cardiac irregularities, usually have a shorter life as well.

I have some doubts as to how it may be determined whether the life span of any human is actually increased with a drug. It would seem to me extending the life of anyone beyond the record, which I beleive is a hundred sixteen years, would only show there is some hope in the process. Of course, if life is as weak and debilitated as many of those who live to great age are, there is some question in my mind if it is worth extending the life at all. Becoming a public charge is hardly something to look forward to, and there is certainly no real feeling of achievement to be gained in having your name entered in the Guinness Book Of Records as having been the oldest person alive, as the entry would occur only once you have died.

I doubt a longevity pill, or an elixir, will be available until long after I have passed on, but I doubt I will be missing much. Further, I doubt the alchemists of the Middle Ages could have extracted these sophisticated organic chemicals, the kind that scientists say are required to extend human life, with their quite limited laboratory apparatus. Having no sense of the sterile atmosphere of the modern chemical laboratory, such delicate chemical operations seem unlikely. A modern chemical laboratory is a thing of precision and beauty, and is quite different from the dank, dark, and often chilled, work places we see in the many illustrations of alchemists in the middle ages.

We must also note that the personal requirements of the person who would become an alchemist are quite different from those required by one who would become a magician. For one thing, while a successful and productive magician may be single, the successful alchemist is always a married man. According to Albert Richard Riedel, 'Frater Alburtus,' who for some time before his death in 1986 operated a school of alchemy in Utah, the alchemist must be married and enjoy a congenial relationship with his wife. I can honestly say, all of the alchemists I have known have been married, and I will add, the one I knew who experienced this loss, sincerely mourned the loss of his wife when death took her first. The death of his wife was also, in the case of the one alchemist of my acquaintance who met this fate, the cessation of his further researches into alchemical mysteries.

A successful alchemist, unlike a successful magician, must strive first to develop their character. A youthful alchemist I once met told me he had made no progress at all in alchemy until he turned from 'puffing,' as he called it, to concentrate on refining his character. 'Puffing' is a term of disparagement, usually cast by others at alchemists, but used by them as an example of those who are idly searching in the alchemical realms without having any true result. This young man, who was in his thirties when I met him, was also happily married.

We must conclude, from the testimony of many sources, the alchemical fabrication of the elixir of life, like making the philosopher's stone, is theoretically quite possible, but in practice, it seems highly unlikely. With this in mind, we must await further discoveries from the realms of medical science, which seem now to have taken over the search for the elixir of life. Perhaps in another fifty years, the scientists will have developed a pill, or some other medicine of this nature, although I sincerely doubt it.

Telemerase

I have recently learned there is an enzyme known as telemerase, which scientists who work in the area believe might be used to rejuvenate the aging cells of the human body. Perhaps alchemist's elixir of life produces this enzyme, or the elixir of life might produce something that causes the human body to begin to produce this enzyme once again, as the natural production of this enzyme is said to fall off after the child is born.

IMMORTALITY

Telemerase adds telemers, tiny stabilizing knots - or caps - at the ends of the chromosomes, which are found in each of the many cells of our body. These telemers are worn away each time the cell replicates itself. The death of cells is apparently caused because the 'tails' of the chromosomes in the cell are gradually reduced as the cells reproduce. Once these tails, the telemers, are weakened or gone the DNA of the chromosome can fray and the cell dies. Additional telemers allow replication of the cell to occur without the usual loss of DNA at the end of the chromosome during replication. Once a child is born, the RNA, which makes the enzyme telemerase in the womb, ceases the production of further telemerase. Theoretically, it seems, that until a child is born it is potentially immortal.

The only difficulty found with using the enzyme telemerase to treat aging is the difficulty of delivering it to the person to be treated. Telemerase is very fragile, and it breaks down in the bloodstream. Furthermore, the enzyme can cause cancer to develop, if it should be applied incorrectly. Most cancers have telemerase within their cellular structure, so their cells are able to reproduce without limit. It would seem that the potential life enhancing potent of telemerase could easily become a deathblow for the person using it.

Genetic Klotho Protein

One genetic marker relating to long life, a protein called klotho, has been identified in both mice and men. Through over dosing mice with this protein, their life span has been increased in the laboratory twenty to thirty percent compared to a control group. In a man, this would be an increase, over the biblical three score and ten, of between fourteen and twenty one years. An astrologer friend once told me the ideal human life span would eighty-four years, as it would mean the person died on their Uranus return. I have no idea why this would be an ideal time to die, but I think if the genetic protein klotho could accomplish this, it would likely be worthwhile. The genetic protein klotho is supposedly an aging-suppression gene, extending the life span of mice when it is plentiful, and accelerating aging in mice when it is in short supply. Of course, this says nothing about its real benefits in extending the lives of men and women.

Scientists have managed to double the life of the nematode worm, by muting the effect of the gene involved in its aging. Other scientists have genetically extended the life of fruit flies to almost three times their normal life span. Rather than dying of old age, the treated flies are said to die of starvation, cause by broken wings and legs, which leave them unable to obtain food. There may be a lesson in this for humans. We shall have to see if there is when the time comes.

At present, the best indicator of a long and healthy life is the age of your parents and grandparents at their death. Even in the Middle Ages, as in the ancient world, there were those who lived to a goodly age. Although it has been said our animal bodies were designed to begin reproducing at about twelve, and perish at twenty, there are many instances of people in the old stone age living to a ripe old age, dying in their sixties or later. This story is told by their bones, which reveal their age at death to the concerned scientist. However, even in the present day, those who live a vital life and are aged a hundred years or more are quite rare.

Immortality and Society

While most religions teach the immortality of the soul, belief in the physical immortality of the body is quite rare. Obviously, the potential for human immortality would bring a great strain on our present social system. The civil authorities in every nation would have difficult regulating such a desired condition as long life. The availability of such a long life to most people would require great changes in the social and legal system, as well in such retirement schemes as social security, annuities, and other financial programs. Of course, such a social change would also present almost insurmountable problems for the religious authorities. While it would be interesting to learn

IMMORTALITY

how the various religions would react to this exciting news, I believe it would be the better part of wisdom to keep far away from the debate.

Immortality Through Living A Good Life

While it may not be possible to attain immortality though practicing a healthy life style, it certainly will go a long way toward insuring a vibrant old age. Those who carefully watch their weight, do not smoke or drink alcohol, and maintain a temperate and un-emotional lifestyle are usually assured of living longer and having a greater degree of vitality in their lives as they age.

The excess of emotionalism which many people display is wearing on their body, should they realize it or not. Thus, excesses of emotionalism are to be avoided, as are the grinding passions of long simmering hate and the intense emotional fire caused by intense flashes of lust. This also means those wishing to live long lives must avoid any emotional confrontations with others, including dedication to any cause demanding their deep emotional involvement.

Vegetarianism is encouraged in some, but not in other people, depending upon their occupation or their place in the world. The more harshly they are required to interface with the world, the less likely a vegetarian diet will suit them. No one ever heard of a vegetarian soldier, as one example.

Those who wish for a long life must consider this at an early age, and turn from many things their society may consider normal. This includes having animalistic thoughts, as well as living an animalistic life. At the same time, the person desiring to live long must not beleive they are missing anything of life. They must be content, and truly feel fulfilled. As thoughts tend to draw the deed, the mind must not desire what it does not wish to have. In this way, a person is supposedly able to live to a great age, maintaining at least some of the vitality found in their youth.

I'm sure many among us, believing such a strict regime would lose them all they find pleasurable in life, would probably pass on the opportunity to extend their lives in this manner. Non the less, however we may deal with it, or whatever we may think of immortality, the subject will always hold charm for people, whether it is actually a real phenomena or not.

49,245   Gr. 8.6

Made in the USA
Lexington, KY
21 April 2012